4001 BABIES' NAMES and their Meanings

Part I: 2000 Babies' Names
Part II: 2001 Unusual Babies' Names

JAMES GLENNON

ROBERT HALE · LONDON

Copyright © 1968 and 1971 by James Glennon
First published in Great Britain 1985
20 19 18

ISBN 0 7090 2451 7

Robert Hale Limited
Clerkenwell House
Clerkenwell Green
London EC1R 0HT

Printed in Great Britain by
St Edmundsbury Press Limited,
Bury St Edmunds, Suffolk

HOW DID NAMES COME ABOUT?

In ancient Greece babies were named on the seventh or the tenth day after birth, and the father chose the name. Usually, the eldest son was called after his paternal grandfather and the younger children named after other relatives.

The early Romans used a threefold system: a prefix to the family name *(praenomen)*, given nine days after birth; the inherited family name *(nomen)*; a nickname *(cognomen)*. Under this system the Roman orator and writer, Cicero, became known as Marcus Tullius Cicero.

In mediaeval times the child's name often had association with some event that took place at the time of its birth, perhaps a festival, a storm or a flood.

Then, about the middle of the 16th Century, the Roman Catholic Church required that at least one of the names given in baptism be that of a canonized saint, and so we meet quite a number of people called Matthew, John, Peter, Andrew, Patrick; Mary, Margaret, Elizabeth, Anne, and Catherine.

Resulting from the use of saints' names came the adaptation of men's names for use by women. For instance, parents who wished their daughter to be placed under the patronage of St John, christened her Joan, or perhaps felt equally secure in winning saintly favour by varying it to Joanne or Joanna.

In the Puritan era Prudence, Faith, Hope, Charity, Patience, and other such virtuous names betokening desirable personal qualities came into fashion which no doubt gave their owners something to live up to.

Actors have been known to call their children after stage characters: Juliet, Olivia, Jessica, Bertram, Talbot, Mortimer. Some musicians, particularly singers, have turned to their favourite opera characters giving their offspring such romantic first names as Isolde, Elsa, Elvira, Mimi, Rudolf, Marcel, Mario, Ottavio.

Flowers, too, have made the selection easier for some mothers and fathers, which meant that little girls found themselves answering to Rose, Violet, Lily, Pansy, or Flora; even Lettice or Lettuce.

There have always been fashions in first names, and fashions are always on the move. Every age produces prominent leaders, soldiers, politicians. From such names as Kitchener, Woodrow, Franklin, Winston, Dwight, Victoria, Edith, Amy, and Amelia we can deduce the approximate year of birth of persons so named.

Some names are widely used in several countries, but spelt and pronounced in the manner of the country. To take an example: John is often called "a good old English name" (John Bull was the typical Englishman), but in Scotland it is Ian, in Ireland Sean, Hans in Germany, Juan in Spain, and Giovanni in Italy.

ABBREVIATIONS RELATING TO ORIGINAL SOURCES OF NAMES

ANG.-SAX.	ANGLO-SAXON	LAT.	LATIN
ARAB.	ARABIAN	LIT.	LITHUANIAN
ARM.	ARMENIAN	MAN.	MANDAEAN
CELT.	CELTIC	N.A. IND.	NORTH
CHIN.	CHINESE		AMERICAN
DAN.	DANISH		INDIAN
ENG.	ENGLISH	NOR.	NORSE
EGYP.	EGYPTIAN	OLD ENG.	OLD ENGLISH
FINN.	FINNISH	OLD FR.	OLD FRENCH
FLEM.	FLEMISH	PERS.	PERSIAN
FR.	FRENCH	PHO.	PHOENICIAN
FRIE.	FRIESIAN	RUS.	RUSSIAN
GAEL.	GAELIC	SANS.	SANSKRIT
GR.	GREEK	SCAN.	SCANDINAVIAN
HAW.	HAWAIIAN	SLAV.	SLAVONIC
HEB.	HEBREW	SPAN.	SPANISH
HIN.	HINDUSTANI	SUD.	SUDANI
HUNG.	HUNGARIAN	TEUT.	TEUTONIC
ICE.	ICELANDIC	TURK.	TURKISH
IT.	ITALIAN	WEL.	WELSH
JAP.	JAPANESE		

GIRLS

AASTA: (Teut.) love

ABIGAIL: (Arab.) father's joy; (Heb.) father of joy

ABNAKI: (N. A. Ind.) morning land

ABRONA: (Lat.) goddess of departures

ACACIA: (Gr.) guileless, innocent

ACANTHA: (Gr.) thorny

ACOLA: (Teut.) cool

ACTIA: (Gr.) ray of light

ADA: (Teut.) happy

ADABEL: (Teut.-Lat.) happy one

ADALIA: (Gr.) not easily understood

ADAMINA: (Heb.) of the earth, mortal; also feminine Scottish form of Adam

ADAR: (Heb.) fire; a Hebrew calendar period

ADARA: (Gr.) a virgin

ADELA: (Gr.) vague; (Teut.) noble

ADELAIDE: (Teut.) noble, princess

ADELINE: (Teut.) of noble bearing or lineage

ADELLBERTA: (Teut.) nobly bright

ADELPHE: (Gr.) beloved sister

ADENA: (Gr.) accepted

ADICIA: (Lat.) unjustly treated; (Gr.) injustice

ADIN: (Heb.) slender; delicate

ADINA: (Heb.) slender, voluptuous

ADIONE: (Lat.) a Roman divinity who presides over movements of travellers

ADNAH: (Heb.) pleasure

ADONICA: (Lat.) sweet

ADORA: (Lat.) one adored; (Gr.) a gift

ADOSINDA: (Teut.) of great strength

6

ADRA: (Span.) in turn

ADRANA: (Gr.) a girl from Ardrea

ADRIANNE: feminine form of Adrian

ADRIENNE: (see Adrianne)

AERON: (Cel.) bright queen

AGADA: (Sans.) healthy

AGALIA: (Gr.) restless

AGATHA: (Gr.) good

AGILA: (Lat.) active in mind and body

AGNELLA: (Gr.) pure

AGNES: (Lat.) lamb, denoting gentleness; (Gr.) chaste, pure

AGNOLA: (Lat.) an angel

AGOKAY: (N.A. Ind.) persevering

AGOLA: (Span.) woman who handles the sails

AH-CY: (Chin.) lovely

AH-KEM: (Chin.) good as gold

AH-LAM: (Chin.) orchid-like

AILEEN: an Irish form of Helen or Helene; from (Gr.) light

AILSA: (Gael.) undiscoverable; a Scottish form of Elsa

AINA: (Scot.) own

AKI: (Jap.) autumn

ALAME: (Span.) like the stately poplar tree

ALATEA: (see Althea)

ALBA: (Lat.) white

ALBERTA: feminine form of Albert

ALCYONE: (Gr.) calm

ALDA: (Teut.) happy, rich

ALDITH, ALDYTH: (Old Eng.) old battle

ALEXANDRA, ALEXANDRINA: (Gr.) help of men; also feminine form of Alexander

ALICE: believed to have evolved from German (Adelaide) and Old French (Aliz); in Latinized form meaning noble, or a princess

ALICIA: a 19th century romanticized form of Alice

ALINA: (Lat.) in a straight line

ALINE: (Teut.) noble; evolved from Adeline

ALISON: (Teut.) a famous war-maid; (Gr.) flower of the Alyssum family

ALMA: (Lat.) benign, loving; (Sans.) spirit mind

ALTHEA: (Gr.) from Alethea,

meaning truth

ALUDRA: (Gr.) a virgin

ALVARA: (Port.) white

ALVINA: (Teut.) elfin friend

ALVIRA: (Teut.) elfin arrow

AMANDA: (Lat.) lovable

AMARA: (Sans.) immortal

AMARANTHA: (Gr.) unfading (as a flower)

AMARYLLIS; (Gr.) refreshing stream; (Lat.) a country girl

AMELIA: (Gr.) energetic

AMILIA: a Scottish form of Emily

AMINE: (Arab.) faithful

AMINTA: (Gr.) I protect

AMITY: (Lat.) friendship

AMY: (Lat.) loved one

AMYNTAS: (Gr.) helper

ANASTASIA: (Gr.) resurrection

ANATOLA: (Gr.) sunrise

ANCITA: (Heb.) grace

ANDEANA: (Span.) walker, a goer

ANDREA: (Gr.) brave

ANDREANA: (Gr.) a man's woman

ANEMONE: (Gr.) frail wind flower

ANGELA: (Gr.) angelic

ANGELINE: (see Angela)

ANGELINA: (see Angela)

ANITA: (Heb.) little Ann

ANN: (Heb.) grace

ANNA, ANNE: (see Ann)

ANNABEL: (Heb.-Lat.) beautiful Anna; also formed of two words, Anna (grace) and Bella (fair)

ANNABELLA, ANNABELLE: variants of Annabel

ANNETTE: French form of Anne

ANNYS: (Gr.) complete

ANTHEA: (Gr.) flowery, or lady of flowers

ANTHELIA: (Gr.) opposite the sun

ANTONIA: (Lat.) inestimable

ANYSIA: (Gr.) complete

ANZONETTA: (Teut.) little one of divine origin

ARCADIA: (Gr.) ideal land of peace, happiness and beauty

ARDANA: (Sans.) restless

ARIADNE: (Gr.) sweet singer

ARIANA: (Lat.-Heb.) song of grace

ARLEEN, ARLENE: (Teut.) a

pledge

ASTA: (Teut.) swift as the wolf

ASTRED: (Gr.) the starry one

ASTRID: (Norse) godly strength

AUDREY: (Teut.) regal counsellor

AUGUSTA: (Lat.) revered; feminine form of Augustine

AUREOLA: (Lat.) golden

AURORA, AURORE: (Lat.) dawn

AVELINE: (Heb.) pleasantness

AVERIL: (Fr.) month of April; name of a 7th century Yorkshire saint

AVIS: (Teut.) a refugee in trouble; also a gipsy name

AYESHA: (Pers.) happy

AZALIA: (Gr.) dry; also name of flower

B

BABETTE: (Gr.) little Barbara

BARBARA: (Gr.) the stranger

BARBETTE: (Gr.) little stranger

BEATRICE, BEATRIX: (Lat.) one who blesses, happiness, bringer of joy

BELA: (Hung.) nobly; (Heb.) God's earth

BELINDA: (Lat.) sinuous like a serpent

BELLA, BELLE: French and Italian form of beautiful; Scottish diminutive of Isabel

BELVINA: (Lat.) fair one

BENITA: (Lat.) blessed one

BERENICE, BERNICE: (Gr.) bringer of victory

BERTHA: (Teut.) bright, or beautiful one

BERTHELDA: (Teut.) bright battlemaid

BERYL: (Pers.) crystal; name of gemstone

BESS, BESSIE, BETH, BETSY: shortened forms of Elizabeth

BETHANEY: (Heb.) home of poverty; house of dates

BEULAH: (Heb.) matronly; she who is married

BEVERLEY: variant of old English name Bevis

9

BIANCA: (Lat.) fair

BIDDY: (Celt.) a goddess; an Irish contraction of Bridget

BLANCH: (Teut.) white

BLANCHE: French form of Blanch

BLANDA: (Lat.) flatterer

BLENDA: (Teut.) dazzling white

BRENDA: (Teut.) a flaming sword

BRIANA: (Teut.) a flame; strong

BRIDGET: (Celt.) strong one; same as Brigid

BRIDGET, BRIGID: (Celt.) strong one

BRONWEN, BRONWYN: (Celt.-Welsh) white breast

BUENA: (Span.) good

BRUNILDA, BRUNHILDE, BRYNHILD: (Teut.) compounded from "brunnia" (corslet) and "hild" (battle); breastplate or battlemaid

CALANDRA: (Gr.) a lark

CALDORA: (Gr.) beautiful gift

CALLENA: (Teut.) talkative

CAMILLA: (Lat.) a freeborn attendant at a sacrifice

CAMILLE: (Gr.) a swift-footed messenger of Diana

CARA: (Celt.) friend

CARITA: (Lat.) charity

CARLOTTA: a form of Charlotte

CARMEL: (Heb.) a vineyard; (Arab.) a field of fruit

CARMELA: (Heb.) of the vineyard

CAROL: (Gael.) melody; popular in modern times (particularly in USA) as a shortened form of Caroline

CAROLINE, CAROLYN: (Teut.) virile

10

CARRIE: English contraction of Caroline

CASSANDRA: (Gr.) one who excites love

CATHIE: Scottish diminutive of Catherine

CECILE, CECILIA, CECILY: variants of Celia

CELIA: (Lat.) heaven; sky

CELOSIA: (Gr.) aflame; name of flower

CHARIS: (Gr.) goodwill; in mythology one of the three graces

CHARLOTTE: (Teut.-Fr.) virile, noble; feminine form of English Charles and Italian Carlo

CHARMA: (Gr.) delight, joy

CHARMIAN: (Gr.) a little joy; Cleopatra's favourite serving maid

CHERRY: (Gr.) beloved

CHERYL: modern usage, probably from fiction

CHLOE: (Gr.) a young green shoot; blooming

CHLORA: (Gr.) freshness of spring; verdure

CHLORIS: (Gr.) blooming,

fresh

CHRISTABEL: (Gr.) anointed one; fair follower of Christ

CHRISTINE, CHRISTINA: (Lat.) messenger or follower of Christ

CRISTY: (Lat.) the anointed

CICILY: (from Cecilia)

CLARA: (Lat.) bright, clear

CLARE, CLARICE, CLARISSA: variants of Clara

CLARENDA: (Lat.) brightening

CLARIBEL: (Lat.) brightly fair

CLARICE, CLARISSA: variants of Clara

CLAUDETTE: (Lat.) little lame one

CLAUDIA: (Lat.) lame

CLAUDINE: French form of Claudia

CLEMATIS: (Gr.) lithe; flower name

CLEMENTINA, CLEMENTINE: (Lat.) merciful, gentle

CLEO: (Gr.) glorious

CLOTHILDA, CLOTHILDE: (Teut.) compound of "hloda" (loud) and "hildi" (battle), battlemaid

11

CLYDINA: (Gr.) glorious one

COCHETA: (N.A. Ind.) the unknown

COLINETTE: (Lat.) little dove

COLLEEN: (Irish) a girl

COLUMBINE: (Lat.) flower name

CONSTANCE: (Lat.) faithful, constant

CORA: (Gr.) a maiden

CORALIE: (Fr.) coral, a modern French invention

CORDELIA: (Celt.) jewel of the sea; (Lat.) warm-hearted

CORINNA: (Gr.) maiden

CORNELIA: (Lat.) enduring; feminine of Cornelius, meaning hornlike

CORONA: (Gr.) a crown

CRESSIDA: (Gr.) faithlessness

CRISPINA: (Lat.) curlyheaded. Probably from "crispus", meaning curled

CYNTHIA: (Gr.) of, or from, Mt Cynthus, signifying lofty

CYRA: (Gr.) lady

DAGMAR: (Teut.) Dane's glory

DAINA: (Teut.) disdainful

DAISY: (Pers.) brightness; (Ang.-Sax.) day's eye. Also late-Victorian pet-name for Margaret

DAI-TAI: (Chin.) lead-boy. In Chinese families of many girls where a boy is hoped for, this name is given to a daughter in the belief that she will be followed by a brother, for whom she has led the way

DAMARIS: (Lat.) gentle

DAPHNE: (Gr.) sweet-smelling laurel or bay tree

DARLENE: (Ang.-Sax.) variant of Darling

DAWN: (Teut.) daybreak; a diminutive of Doreen

DEBORAH: (Heb.) a bee, or

queen bee; she rules

DECIMA: (Lat.) the tenth, or tenth girl in order of birth

DEIRDRE: (Celt.) sorrow or doubtful

DELIA: (Gr.) of the island of Delos

DELLA: (Teut.) noble

DELMAR: (Teut.) dweller by the sea

DENISE: (Gr.) of Dionysius; feminine form of Denis

DESDEMONA: (Span.) literally, from a monkey. (Wife of Othello in Shakespeare's play of that name.)

DESIREE: (Lat.) desire, from "desiderata", meaning desired. French form is Désirée

DIANA: (Lat.) moon goddess

DINAH: (Heb.) from law-suit; judged, avenged, vindicated

DISA: (Teut.) active spirit

DOBRANA: (Slav.) good

DOLLY: English contraction of Dorothea

DOLORES: (Lat.) lady of sorrows; (Span.) Mary of the sorrows

DONNA: (Span.) lady

DORA: (Gr.) a gift; also a diminutive of Dorothea and Dorothy

DORCAS: (Gr.) a gazelle

DOREEN: (Fr.) the gilded; probably an Irish form of Dorothy

DORETTE: (Gr.) little gift

DORINDA: (Gr.) given

DORIS: (Gr.) a sacrificial knife

DOROTHEA, DOROTHY: (Gr.) gift of God

DRUSILLA: (Gr.) watered by the dew; (Lat.) strong

DUANA: (Celt.) a song

DULCINEA: (Lat.) sweet one

DULCY, DULCIE: English contractions of Dulcibella, from Latin "dulcis", meaning sweet

DURETTA: (Span.) little steadfast one

DYMPHNA: (Celt.) white wave

DYNA: (Gr.) power

DYOTA: (Sans.) light, sunshine

EARLENE: (Teut.) a noble-woman of high rank

EBERTA: (Teut.) of bright mind

EDA: see Edith

EDANA, EDENA, EDEVA: early forms of Edith

EDIA: (Teut.) rich friend

EDITH: (Ang.-Sax.) happy; (Teut.) rich gift. This name has been known in a Latin-ized form, "Ediva"; also in England and other parts as Eda, Edie, Edine, Edithe

EDLYN: (Teut.) rich gentle-woman

EDNA: source unknown, but may have come from (Teut.) rich counsellor, or (Heb.) pleasure, perfect happiness

EDNAN: (Heb.) pleasure

EDWINA: a modern female form of Edwin

EEREENA: (Gr.) messenger of peace

EFFIE: a diminutive of Euphemia

EGLON: (Heb.) the gentle

EILEEN: (Gr.) a torch, a variant of Helen and Eileen. Also spelt Aileen

ELA: (Norse) holy

ELAIN, ELAINE: from (Gr.) a torch; variants of Helen

ELEANOR, ELEANORA, ELI-NOR: (Gr.) light; same as Helen, Helene

ELFREDA, ELFRIDA: Old English compound of "aelf" (elf) and "thryth" (strength)

ELIDA: (Lat.) the excluded

ELISSA: see Elizabeth

ELISABETH, ELIZABETH: (Heb.) God's oath; conse-crated to God

ELLA: (Teut.) gift of the elf

ELLAMAE: (Teut.) elfin kins-woman

ELLEN: (Gr.) a torch. Also another form of Eleanor and Helen

ELLENIS: (Gr.) the original spelling of Helene, preceded by an aspirate

ELMA: (Gr.) love

ELOISA: (Teut.) celebrated holiness

ELOISE: same as Eloisa

ELPHIA: (Gr.) ivory

ELSA: German derivative of Elisabeth. More commonly used after heroine in Wagner's opera "Lohengrin"

ELSIE: English diminutive of Elizabeth

ELSPETH: Scottish diminutive of Elizabeth

ELVA: (Teut.) elfin

ELVIRA: (Lat.) white; later popular in Spain

EMILIA: a variant of Emily

EMILY: derived from Emeline and Emmeline, meaning (Lat.-Teut.) industrious

EMMA: (Teut.) signifying greatness. Old German form meaning whole or universal

ENA: modern usage, probably English form of Irish Eithne

ENID: (Celt.) purity

ERICA: (Gr.) heather blossom; (Teut.) mighty heroine

ERINA: (Gael.) of Ireland; Irish girl

ERMENTRUD, ERMYNTRUDE: (Teut.) loyal maiden (of a nation)

ERMINIA: (Lat.) regal

ERNA: (Ang.-Sax.) retiring

ERNESTINE: feminine form of Ernest, earnestness

ESME: diminutive of Esmeralda

ESMERELDA: (Span.) emerald

ESSIE: (Pers.) star. Also diminutive of Esther

ESTELLE: (Fr.) form of Stella

ESTERA: (Luo) star

ESTHER: generally supposed to come from the Persian word meaning star. The Old Testament gives it as Persian equivalent of the Hebrew "Hadassah", myrtle

ESTRA: (Lat.) alien

ETHEL: (Teut.) noble, or noble birth

ETHELREDA: (Teut.) noble counsellor

15

ETHELWYN: (Teut.) noble friend

ETTA: (Teut.) ruler of the home

EUDORA: (Gr.) happy gift

EUGENIA, EUGENIE: (Gr.) nobly born

EULALIA, EULALIE: (Gr.) of fair speech

EUNICE: (Gr.) happily victorious

EUPHEMIA, EUPHEMIE: (Gr.) speaker of words of good omen

EUPHRASIA, EUPHRASIE: (Gr.) joyful

EVA: see Eve

EVANGELINE: (Gr.) bringer of good news

EVE: (Heb.) life; lively

EVELEEN: Irish diminutive of Eva

EXILDA: (Teut.) banished; (Lat.) the exiled

FAIRLIE: (Eng.) pet-name for Felicity

FAITH: (Teut.) unwavering trust. Popular in Puritan times

FALDA: (Ice.) folded wings

FANIA: Slavonic form of Frances

FANNY: a diminutive of Frances

FAY, FAYE: (Old Fr.) fidelity, or faithful one; also fairy

FEDORA: (Gr.) gift of God

FELICIA: variant of Felicity

FELICITY: (Lat.) happiness

FELITA: (Lat.) happy little one

FIDELIA: (Lat.) faithful one

FIDONIA: (Gr.) thrifty

FILMA: (Teut.) misty, hazy

FILOMENA: (Lat.) daughter of light

FINETTE: (Heb.) little addition

FIONA: thought to have been invented by William Sharp for his literary character Fiona Macleod, or derived from Gaelic "fionn", fair, white

FLAVIA: (Lat.) blonde girl

FLAVILLA: (Lat.) yellow hair

FLEURETTE: (Fr.) little flower

FLO: a contraction of Flora or Florence

FLORA: (Lat.) flowers; in mythology, goddess of flowers

FLORENCE: (Lat.) blooming; flourishing

FLORIAN: (Lat.) flowery

FLORINDA: Spanish form of Flora

FLORIS: (Lat.) a flower

FRANCES: (Teut.) free

FRANCIS: (Fr.) French or Frankish

FREDA: a diminutive of Winifred

FREDERICA: (Teut.) peaceful ruler; feminine of Frederick

FRONIA: (Gr.) a thinker

GABRIELLE: (Heb.) heroine of God

GAIL: a contraction of Abigail

GALATEA: (Gr.) milk-white. In Greek mythology, a sea nymph who loved Acis

GALATIA: (Gr.) laughing girl

GARDA: (Teut.) prepared

GENEVIEVE: (Celt.) white wave

GENEVRA: an English contraction of Genevieve

GEORGETTE: a French diminutive of George

GEORGINA: (Gr.) husband-woman; derivative of George

GERALDINE: (Teut.) fair battlemaid; feminine form of Gerald

GERDA: (Teut.) girdled

GERTRUDE: (Teut.) spear maid

17

GILDA: (Ang.-Sax.) golden; (Celt.) God's servant

GILLIAN: English form of Julia

GIRALDA: (Teut.) powerful contendant; Italian form of Geraldine

GISELLE: (Teut.) a hostage

GLADYS: Welsh form of Latin Claudia. Also Gwladys

GLENDORA: (Teut.-Gr.) gift of the glen

GLENICE, GLENYSS: (Gael.) from the mountain glen

GLORIA: (Lat.) glory

GODIVA: (Teut.) divine gift. "Godgifu" (Latinized as Godiva) was heroine of the 11th century Coventry legend

GONDOLINE: (Teut.) wise, brave one

GRACE: (Lat.) elegance, or beauty of form and movement

GRACIENNE: (Lat.) little one

GRETA: Swedish abbreviation of Margaret

GRETCHEN: (Pers.) pearl. A German contraction of Margaret

GWEN, GWENDA: abbreviations of Gwendolen

GWENDOLEN: (Celt.) white-bow

GWYNETH: (Celt.) blessed

GYNETH: (Celt.) fair one

HAGAR: (Heb.) timid stranger; flight

HAIDEE: (Gr.) modest

HAIMA: (Sans.) made of gold

HANNAH: (Heb.) favoured of God

HAZEL: (Teut.) brown; (Heb.) protected by God

HEATHER: (Teut.) a beautiful flowering shrub. A favourite Scottish name

HEDIA: (Gr.) pleasing

HELEN, HELENA: (Gr.) light

HELGA: (Gr.) holy

HELOISE: (Teut.) some references give it as (Teut.)

famous warrior; others a variant of Helewidis from "haila", sound and "vid", wide

HELVITIA: (Lat.) high hill dwelling

HENRIETTA, HENRIETTE: (Teut.) ruler of the home. Also female form of Henry

HEPHZIBAH: (Heb.) my delight is in her. Name of wife of Hezekiah

HERMIONE: (Lat.) kindred; maid of high degree

HERTHA: (Teut.) goddess of fertility

HESTER, HESTHER: see Ester

HETTY: English diminutive of Harriet

HILARY: (Lat.) cheerful, merry

HILDA: (Teut.) battlemaid

HILDEGARDE: (Teut.) protecting battlemaid

HOHOKA: (N.A. Ind.) wild dove

HONOR, HONORA, HONORIA: (Lat.) reputation; sense of what is right and true

HOPE: (Ang.-Sax.) trust; expectation of good

HORTENSE, HORTENSIA: (Lat.) at home in a garden

HOWIN: (Chin.) a loyal swallow

HULDA: (Norse) muffled; covered

HULDAH: (Heb.) weasel

HULLE: (Dutch) veiled

HYACINTH: (Gr.) flower of the royal purple; (Lat.) sapphire

HYPATIA: (Gr.) superior

IANESSA: (Gr.) gentle ruler

IANTHE: (Gr.) the violet, symbol of modesty

IDA: (Gr.) happy

IDALIA: (Gr.) happiness

IDETTE: (Gr.) happy little one

ILKA: (Gael.) every

ILYTHIA: (Gr.) goddess presiding over childbirth

IMELDA: (Old Eng.) the moderate one

IMOGEN: (Gr.) beloved child

INES: (Gr.) a daughter

INEX: (Gr.) pure. Portuguese form of Agnes

INGRID: (Scand.) maiden of the Ingvaeones

IRENE: (Gr.) peace; messenger of peace

IRIS: (Gr.) the rainbow; (Lat.) goddess of the rainbow

ISA: (Teut.) with a spirit like iron

ISABEL, ISABELLA: other forms of Elizabeth

ISEULT: (Celt.) fair

ISOLDE: see Iseult

ISOTTA: (Celt.) the fair

IVY: (Teut.) a clinging vin constancy

IXIA: (Gr.) the mistletoe

IZORA: (Arab.) dawn

JACINTH: name of precious stone, probably from (Gr.) hyacinth

JACINT(H)A: (Gr.) wearer of the purple

JACQUELINE: (Heb.) the supplanter

JAHOLA: (Heb.) a dove

JANE: (Heb.) grace of God; feminine form of John

JANET: (Heb.) little one of divine grace

JEAN: Scottish form of Jane, Joan, or Johanna

JEMINA: (Arab.) the doer; (Heb.) a dove

JENNIFER: (Celt.) white phantom or white wave

JENNY: pet-name for Jane and Jennifer

JESSICA: (Heb.) He beholds, or God's grace

JESSIE: form of Janet, chiefly Scots

JILL: pet-form of Gillian and Julia

JOAN: see Jane

JOANNA, JOHANNA: (Heb.) grace of the Lord

JOCELIN, JOCELYN: (Lat.) playful

JOLETTA: (Lat.) the violet, symbol of modesty.

JOSEPHINE: French feminine derivative of Joseph

JOY: (Teut.) pleasure; (Lat.) gladness, a jewel

JOYCE: (Teut.) to enjoy; (Lat.) merry; a Celtic name of saint

JOYLEEN: modern usage

JOYVITA: (Lat.) jovial

JUANITA: Spanish form of Jane

JUDITH: (Heb.) praised of the Lord; a Jewess

JUDY: English contraction of Judith

JULIA: (Lat.) downy-face, feminine form of Julius

JULIANA: Spanish form of Julia

JULIET, JULIETTE: other forms of Julia. Shakespeare took it from Italian Giuliette, from Giulia, or Julia

JUN: (Chin.) truth; (Jap.) obedient

JUNE: (Lat.) ever faithful; from the goddess Juno

KALDORA: (Gr.) beautiful gift

KALWA: (Finn.) heroic

KANE: (Jap.) golden

KARABEL: (Span.) beautiful face

KAREN: Danish form of Katherine

KARENA: (Gr.) pure

KARINA: Swedish form of Katherine

KATE: a contraction of Katherine

KATHARINE, KATHERINE, CATHARINE, CATHERINE: (Gr.) pure, name of virgin martyr of Alexandria

KATHINI: (Kikuyu) little bird

KATHLEEN: (Celt.) beautiful eyes; also Irish form of Katherine

KATHRYN, KATRINE: variants of Katherine

KATINKA: Russian form of Katherine

KAY: (Gr.) I rejoice

KELDA: (Scan.) a spring or fountain

KERRY: (provincial English) a large apron

KIN: (Jap.) golden

KIRSTY: (Gr.) Christian. Scottish contraction of Christina

KITTY: a contraction of Katherine

KUKI: (Jap.) snow

KUNI: (Jap.) country born

KWAI: (Chin.) fragrance of a rose

KWONG: (Chin.) broad

LALA: (Slav.) the tulip

LALLA: (Scottish) of the lowlands; used by Thomas Moore for his poem, "Lalla Rookh" (1817)

LAURA: (Lat.) the laurel. Latin form of Laurence

LAURETTE: (Lat.) little victorious one

LAURINDA: a variant of Laura

LAVINIA: (Lat.) the cleansed. Name of daughter of Latinus, the second wife of Aeneas

LEAH: (Lat.) weary; (Heb.) cow

LEE: (Chin.) plum

LEILA: (Arab.-Pers.) dark, or dark oriental beauty

LELIA: (Teut.) loyal

LENA: a diminutive of Helen(a)

LENTULA: (Celt.) mild

LEONIE: French form of Leon; feminine form of Leo

LEONORA: (Gr.) light. Leonora the Italian, Leonore the French, Lenore the German forms

LESLEY: feminine form of Leslie

LETTICE, LAETITIA: from Latin, meaning gladness

LETTY: a variant of Lettice

LEYLA: (Arab.) night

LIAN: (Chin.) graceful willow

LIBBY: an English contraction of Elizabeth

LIDA: (Slav.) people's love

LILA: (Pers.) lilac

LILIAN, LILIAS: (Lat.) lily, purity

LILITH: (Heb.) a serpent, the Assyrian goddess of night

LILY: (Lat.) the bloom; (Gr.) symbol of purity

LINDA: (Lat.) handsome; a contraction of Belinda

LINNET: (Celt.) shapely

LIRIA: (Gr.) delicate

LISA, LISE, LIZA, LIZZIE: contractions of Elizabeth

LOIS: (Gr.) desirable, good

LOLA: (Teut.) virile. A Spanish diminutive of Dolores; (Lat.) sorrows

LOLETA: (Span.) maid of the sorrows

LORINDA: (Lat.) the learned; another form of Laura

LORNA: a feminine form of Lorn(e); from the Ang.-Sax. lost

LORRAINE: derived from the province of Lorraine

LOTTIE, LOTTY: English diminutives of Charlotte

LOUELLA: (Teut.) shrewd war heroine

LOUISA, LOUISE: (Teut.) war heroine; feminine variants of Louis

LUCIA: (Lat.) light, daybreak

LUCIANNA: (Lat.) gracious gift

LUCINDA: (Lat.) shining, clear

LUCILLE: (Lat.) light-shedding

LUCRECE, LUCRETIA: (Lat.) born at dawn

LUCY: (Lat.) born at daybreak; feminine form of Lucius

LULU: (N.A. Ind.) a rabbit; (Pers.) a jewel

LUNEDA: (Celt.) shapely

LYDIA: (Gr.) a maid of Lydia

LYNETTE: see Linnet

MABEL: (Celt.) mirth; the English form of Amabel

MADELINE, MAGDALEN:
(Heb.) woman of Magdala;
name much used after sup-
posed discovery of relics of
St Mary Magdalene in 13th
century

MADGE: English contraction
of Margaret

MAGDALENE: see Madeline

MAGGIE: Scottish form of
Margaret

MAHALA: (Heb.) sweet singer;
(N.A. Ind.) woman

MAIRE: Irish form of Mary

MAISIE: Scottish diminutive
of Margaret

MALVINA: (Gael.) from
"maol-mhin" meaning
smooth brow

MAMIE: an American diminutive of Mary

MANDY: a modern form of
Amanda

MARCELLA: (Teut.) a semi-
precious pink stone, named
after St Marcel of Piedmont;
feminine form of Marcellus

MARCIA: (Latin) brave, derived from god Mars

MARGARET: (Gr.) a pearl

MARGARETE: a Swiss form of
Margaret

MARGARITA: a Spanish form
of Margaret

MARGERY, MARJORIE: other
forms of Margaret

MARIA: Latin form of Mary.
Universal throughout Europe;
came into fashion in England
in 18th century

MARIE: French form of Mary

**MARIAN, MARIANNE, MARY-
ANN:** a compound of Mary
and Anne

MARLENE: (Heb.) of Magdala

MARTHA: (Arab.) a lady

MARTINA: feminine of Martin

MARY: (Heb.) wished-for child.
The name of the Blessed
Virgin, and as such was
once considered too sacred
for common use; first found
as Christian name in Eng-
land at end of 12th century

MARYLYN: (Heb.) of Mary's
line

MATHILDA, MATILDA: (Teut.)
mighty battlemaid, heroine

MATSU: (Jap.) pine tree

MAUD, MAUDE: contractions

of Matilda

MAUREEN: (Celt.) dark; also Irish form of Mary

MAVIS: (Celt.) the song-thrush

MAY: (Teut.) the month; a maiden; a 19th-century pet-form of Margaret

MAYBELLE: (Teut.) beautiful May

MEG: an English contraction of Margaret

MEGAN: (Lat.) great

MELANIE: (Lat.) black, or one in black—a mourner

MELINA: (Lat.) honey-sweet

MELLIE: (Gr.) sweet

MELLITA: (Gr.) honeyed

MELISSA: (Gr.) bee, a symbol of industry

MELVA: (Celt.) chief

MELVINA: a variant of Melva

MENA: (Lat.) mercy

MERCY: compassion: a popular Puritan name

MEREDITH: (Celt.) sea-protector

MERLE: (Lat.) a blackbird

MILBURGA: (Teut.) mild pledge

MILDRED: (Gr.) mild power

MILLICENT: (Lat.) sweet singer; (Gr.) goddess of moisture

MILLIE: English contraction of Millicent

MIMI: (Teut.) resolute opponent

MINA: pet-name for Wilhelmina

MINDORA: (Teut.) love's gift

MINNA: (Teut.) love, memory

MINNIE: (Teut.) remembrance; Scottish form of Mary

MIRA, MYRA: (Slav.) peace; (Gr.) she who weeps

MIRANDA: (Lat.) admirable

MIRIAM: (Heb.) exalted; also wished-for child

MOCITA: (Sans.) set free

MOIRA: (Gr.) destiny; (Celt.) gentle

MOLL, MOLLIE, MOLLY: English contractions of Mary

MONA: (Teut.) lonely, or remote; (Lat.) celibate

MONICA: (Lat.) advisor

MORNA: (Celt.) beloved

MOTO: (Jap.) source

MURIEL: (Gr.) fragrant, perfumed; the myrrh

MYRA: see Mira
MYRNA: modern usage
MYRTLE: (Gr.) token of victory

NADA: (Sans.) a species of reed
NADINE: (Slav.) hope
NAIDA: (Lat.) water nymph
NAMI: (Jap.) wave
NAN: abbreviation of Nancy
NANCY: (Heb.) grace; another form of Anne
NANETTE: (Heb.) little graceful one; also French form of Nancy
NAOMI: (Heb.) pleasantness, or pleasant one
NATALIE: (Lat.) Christmas child
NATSU: (Jap.) summer
NELL, NELLIE, NELLY: variants of Ellen, Eleanor, or Helen

NERINE: (Gr.) sea-born; a flower
NERISSA: (Gr.) of the sea
NESSIE: Welsh diminutive of Agnes
NESTA: variant of Nessie
NICOLETTE: (Gr.) victorious little one
NIETA: (Span.) granddaughter
NINA: (Babylonian) in mythology a goddess of the sea
NITA: a Spanish contraction of Juanita
NOELEEN: modern usage
NOELLA, NOELLE: (Teut.) the Nativity; born on Christmas Day
NORA, NORAH: (Lat.) honour; Irish abbreviated form of Honora
NOREEN: an Irish variant of Nora
NORIA: (Pers.) a water-wheel
NORMA: origin obscure, but may have derived from Latin meaning exact to a pattern or precept. More generally used after Bellini's opera, "Norma" (1831)

O

OCTAVIA: (Lat.) the eighth
ODETTE: (Teut.) heritage
OLGA: Russian name of Scandinavian origin, "helga"
OLIVE, OLIVIA: the olive tree, symbol of peace, feminine form of Oliver
OLYMPIA: (Gr.) of (Mt) Olympus; high, heavenly
ORIOLA: (Lat.) the oriole
ORTRUD: (Teut.) golden maid
OUIDA: modern usage, probably coined from nom-de-plume of once-popular novelist

P

PAMELA: (Teut.) gift of the elf, suggesting intellect

PANDORA: (Gr.) all-gifted; universal gift
PANSY: (Gr.) remembrance
PANTHIA: (Gr.) divine
PATIENCE: (Lat.) calm endurance
PAT, PATTIE, PATTY: see Patricia
PATRICIA: (Lat.) of noble birth; feminine form of Patrick
PAULA: (Lat.) little; feminine form of Paul
PAULETTE: (Lat.) a little wee one
PAULINA, PAULINE: (Lat.) little one
PEARL: probably a variant of Latin word "perula", pear; also coined after name of gem
PEGGY: Old English diminutive of Margaret
PENELOPE: (Gr.) a weaver
PERDITA: (Lat.) lost
PETRINA: (Gr.-Lat.) stony
PETRONELLA: (Lat.) from the Gentile name Petronius
PHEBE, PHOEBE: (Gr.) the shining one

PHILIPPA: (Gr.) lover of horses

PHILOMENA: (Gr.) I am loved; loving mind

PHYLLIS, PHILLIS, PHILLIDA: (Gr.) a leafy green bough

PILAR: (Lat.) tall and strong (like a pillar)

POLL, POLLY: variants of Mary

POPPY: Old English after name of flower

PRIMROSE: (Lat.) first rose

PRISCILLA: (Lat.) old, indicating a long life

PRUDENCE: (Lat.) prudent

PSYCHE: (Gr.) the soul, emphasizing the spiritual nature

QUEENA: (Teut.) consort of a king; female sovereign

QUENBY: (Scan.) womanly

QUINTILLA: (Lat.) the fifth girl; a Roman prophetess

RACHEL: (Heb.) a ewe, or ewe lamb

RAE: a contraction of Rachel

RAELEAN, RAELEEN, RAELINE: modern usage: coined by someone with an ear for something prettily new, and borrowed by many in the 1960s

RAMONA: (Teut.) under judge's protection; also a Spanish name

RAPHAELA: (Heb.) God's health

REBECCA, REBEKAH: possibly from Hebrew word meaning "heifer"; other authorities give meaning as peacemaker, and one of enchanting beauty

REGINA: (Lat.) queen; (Teut.) purity, purified. Revived in England in 19th century

RENATA: (Lat.) born again

28

RENITA: (Lat.) resistance

RHODA: (Gr.) a rose

RINA: (Gr.) pure; probably also variant of Rinnah

RINNAH: (Heb.) a ringing cry

RITA: (Sans.) brave, honest; also contraction of Margaret and Margarita

ROBERTA: (Teut.) bright flame; feminine form of Robert

ROMA: (Romany) a gipsy; also Italian spelling of city of Rome

ROMOLA: (Lat.) a Roman lady

ROSA: Latinized version of Rose

ROSABEL: (Lat.) beautiful rose

ROSALEEN: (Lat.) noble rose

ROSALIE: (Lat.) little rose

ROSALIND, ROSALINDA, ROSALINE: variants of Rose

ROSAMUND: (Teut.) horse-protection; (Lat.) rose of the world

ROSANNE: (Lat.-Heb.) rose of grace

ROSE: origin obscure, although thought to have derived from "(h)ros", or horse, and introduced into England by the Normans in the form of Roese; for centuries identified with the flower

ROSETTA: (Lat.) little rose

ROSEMARY: (Lat.-Heb.) Mary's rose; dew of the sea

ROWENA: (Celt.) white-bosomed

ROXANA, ROXANE: (Pers.) dawn of day

RUBY: a gem; thought to have derived from Rupert, meaning bright flame

RUTH: origin obscure; may have derived from Hebrew word meaning a vision; first used in England after the Reformation

SABINA: (Lat.) a Sabine woman (the Sabines of ancient Italy dwelt in mountains beyond the Tiber)

SABRINA: (Old Eng.) legendary daughter of Loerine, mythical king of England

SADIE: an English pet-name for Sarah

SALLY: an English contraction of Sarah, but has become an independent name

SALOME: (Heb.) peaceable

SALVINA: (Lat.) the sage flower; symbol of caution

SAMANTHA: origin obscure

SANDRA: derivative of Alexandra and Cassandra

SARA(H): (Heb.) princess

SARAID: (Celt.) excellent; used in Ireland

SAVANNAH: (Ang.-Sax.) a treeless plain

SELENA, SELINA: (Gr.) the moon; moonlight

SELMA: (Celt.) fair

SERENA: (Lat.) tranquil; calm

SHEELAGH, SHEILA: Irish forms of Cecilia

SHIRLEY: (Teut.) meadow; sweet

SIBYL: (Gr.) a wise woman

SIGRID: (Teut.) conquering counsellor

SILVIA, SYLVIA: (Lat.) forest dweller

SOLVEIG: (Ice.) sunshine·

SOPHIA, SOPHIE, SONIA: (Gr.) wisdom

SUSAN(NAH): (Heb.) white lily

SUZETTE: (Heb.) little lily

SYLVIA: see Sibyl

TABITHA: (Aramaic) graceful gazelle; (Syrian) gazelle

TAMARA: (East Indian) aspiration

TERESA, THERESA: (Gr.) reap; a carrier of corn

TERESE: (Teut.) huntress

TESS (A): see Terese

THALIA: (Gr.) luxuriant bloom

THEA: (Gr.) Divine; a contraction of Theodora

THECLA: (Gr.) Divine fame

THELMA: (Gr.) a nursling

THEODORA: feminine of Theodore

THEODOSIA: (Gr.) divinely given

THIRZA: (Heb.) pleasantness

THORA: (Teut.) born of thunder

THYRA: (Teut.) belonging to Tyr, the Scandinavian god of battles

TIFFANY: (Gr.) divine manifestation

TRACY: from the surname

TRIX, TRIXIE: contractions of Beatrice, or Beatrix

TRUDY: (Eng.) Contraction of Gertrude

TRYPHENA: (Gr.) daintiness, delicacy

UDA: (Teut.) rich

ULRICA: (Teut.) noble ruler; rich

UNA: (Lat.) the one, expressive of perfection

URANIA: (Gr.) heavenly; in mythology muse of astronomy, daughter of Jupiter and Mnemosyne

URSA: (Lat.) of distinguished quality; the she-bear

URSULA: (Lat.) variant of Ursa

VALERIE: (Lat.) valiant, strong

VANESSA: (Gr.) a butterfly

VANITA: (Sans.) wished for, desired

VANORA: (Celt.) white wave

VENETIA: (Lat.) blessed

VERA: (Lat.) truth, also Russian form of faith

VERNA: (Lat.) vernal, pertaining to spring

VERNITA: (Lat.) little blooming one

VERONA: (Lat.) the truthful

VERONICA: (Lat.-Gr.) true image

VESTA: (Gr.) same as Hestia; goddess of fire and of the family hearth

VICTORIA: (Lat.) victorious; feminine form of Victor

VIDA: (Heb.) beloved; (Lat.) life

VIOLA: see Violante

VIOLANTE: (Lat.) the violet, symbol of modesty

VIOLET: (Lat.) modest grace

VIOLETTA: (Lat.) little violet

VIRGINIA: (Lat.) a maid, virgin

VIVIAN: (Lat.) animated

VIVIENNE: French form of Vivian

WAHLENE: (Teut.) chosen

WANDA: (Teut.) shepherdess

WINIFRED: (Teut.) friend of peace

WINNY: (Celt.) famine; (Teut.) friend

WYLDA: (Teut.) wayward

WYLMA: (Teut.) resolute contender

XENE: (Gr.) a woman guest

XAVERIE: (Arab.) bird

XYLINA: (Gr.) wood dweller

YOLANDE: French form of Yolante (Gr.) violet of the land

YSEULT, ISOLT: (Celt.) a picture fair

YVETTE: (Teut.) little ivy vine

YVONNE: (Heb.) grace of the Lord. French feminine of Ivon

of the East; sunrise

ZELOSA: (Gr.) jealous

ZENOBIA: (Arab.) her father's ornament

ZERLINDA: (Heb.-Lat.) a beautiful dawn

ZILLAH: (Heb.) a shadow

ZIONA: (Heb.) a hill

ZOE: (Gr.) life

ZORA: (Arab.) dawn

ZADIE: (Arab.) affluent

ZARA(H): (Arab.) brightness

33

BOYS

AARON: (Heb.) lofty mountain; inspired; descended from the gods

ABE, ABY: contractions of Abraham

ABEL: (Heb.) a breath, vapour, vanity; second son of Adam and Eve

ABELARD: (Teut.) of noble firmness

ABNER: (Heb.) father of light

ABRAHAM: (Heb.) father of a multitude; originally Abram, high father

ABSALOM: (Heb.) father of peace

ACHILLE: French form of Achilles

ACHILLES: (Gr.) without lips; Greek hero and central figure of Homer's "Iliad"

ADAM: (Heb.) red earth man; first man

ADELBERT: (Teut.) nobly bright

ADOLF, ADOLPH: (Teut.) noble wolf

ADOLPHUS: Latin form of Adolf

ADRIAN: (Lat.) of Adria

AINSLEY: (Gael.) his own (ain) self

ALAN, ALLAN: (Celt.) harmony; (Gael.) fair, handsome

ALARIC: (Gothic) all ruler

ALASTAIR: (Gr.) avenger; original Gaelic Alasdair, also variant of Alister

ALBERT: (Teut.) nobly bright

ALECK, ALEX, ALICK: contractions of Alexander

ALEXANDER: (Gr.) defender, helper of men

ALEXIS: (Gr.) defender, helper

ALFRED: (Teut.) counsellor

ALGAR: (Old Eng.) elf spear

ALGERNON: (Old Fr.) bearded

ALGY: contraction of Algernon

ALISTER: (Gr.) avenger, defender of men

ALLAN: see Alan

ALLYN: see Alan

ALMERICK: (Teut.) work ruler

ALONZO: (Teut.) friend of all

ALOYSIUS: (Teut.) famous warrior; 16th century Spanish saint

ALPHONSO: (Teut.) eager for the fray, willing

ALVAN, ALVIN: (Teut.) beloved of all

ALWIN, ALWYN: variants of Alvan

AMBROSE: (Gr.) immortal

AMOS: (Gr.) bearer of burdens; courageous

ANDREW: (Gr.) manly, brave

ANGUS: (Celt.) excellent virtue

ANSELM: (Teut.) divine helmet, protection

ANTHONY, ANTONY: (Lat.) priceless, highly praised

ANTOL: (Hung.) estimable

ANTON: Slav. form of Anthony

ARCHER: (Teut.) a bowman

ARCHIBALD: (Teut.) very bold, bold archer

ARNOLD: (Teut.) strong as an eagle

ARTHUR: (Celt.) lofty, noble; (Cymric) bearman

ARVIN: (Teut.) man of the people

ASA: (Heb.) healer

ASHER: (Heb.) blessed, fortunate; (Egypt.) evening

ATHOL: (Teut.) of noble ancestry; (Ang.-Sax.) noble stone

AUBREY: (Lat.) fair chief

AUDLEY: (Teut.) undefined

AUGUSTIN, AUGUSTUS: (Lat.) venerable, consecrated

AUSTIN: an English contraction of Augustin

AVERIA: (Teut.) assertive

AYLMER: (Teut.) of noble fame

AYLWARD: (Teut.) formidable guard

AYLWIN: (Teut.) devoted friend

BALDWIN: (Teut.) bold friend

BALFOUR: (Gael.) pasture ground

BARNABAS: (Heb.) consoling son

BARNABY: Teutonic form of Barnabas

BARNARD: (Teut.) firm commander

BARNY: an Irish contraction of Bernard

BARRY: (Celt.) he who looks straight at the mark; good marksman

BARTHOLOMEW: (Heb.) son of furrows; farmer

BARTRAM: (Teut.) fortunate farmer

BASIL: (Gr.) kingly

BEAUMONT: (Old Fr.) beautiful height; fair hill

BENEDICT: (Lat.) blessed

BENJAMIN: (Heb.) son of my strength; son of my right hand

BERESFORD: dweller by the bear's ford

BERKLEY: (Teut.) dweller at the birch meadow

BERMAN: (Teut.) bear keeper

BERNARD: (Teut.) bold as a bear

BERT: contraction of Bertram, Albert, and Herbert

BERTRAM: illustrious one; bright raven

BERTWIN: (Teut.) illustrious friend

BEVERLEY: (Ang.-Sax.) from the beaver meadow

BILL, BILLY: contractions of William

BLAINE: (Old Eng.) a bubble

BLAIR: (Teut.) dweller on a plain; (Gael.) a battleground

BLAISE: (Lat.) babbler

BLAKE: (Teut.) as opposed to pallid

BLAND: (Lat.) gentle

BOB: English and Scottish contraction of Robert

BONAR: (Lat.) good
BONIFACE: (Lat.) doer of good; benefactor
BORDEN: (Old Eng.) refrain of a song
BORIS: (Rus.) fighter
BOURNE: (Old Fr.) destiny
BOWMAN: (Old Eng.) archer
BOYCE: modern usage
BOYD: (Celt.) yellow-haired
BOYDELL: (Celt.) wise fair one
BOYLE: (Teut.) agitation
BRADEN: (Teut.) broad
BRADLEY: (Teut.) dweller in a broad meadow
BRADY: (Gr.) slow
BRAND: (Teut.) a flaming sword
BRANDON: (Teut.) firebrand
BRANT: (Teut.) a flaming ray
BRENDAN: (Teut.) aflame
BRETT: (Gael.) upright
BREVIS: (Lat.) short, frugal
BREWSTER: (Old Eng.) one who brews
BRIAN, BRIANT: (Celt.) strong; (Gael.) in a position of dignity
BRICE: (Ang.-Sax.) breach

BRION: (Gael.) nobly descended
BRISBANE: (Gael.) royal mount
BRODERICK: (Teut.) the king's tormentor
BRODIE: (Teut.) a goad
BROMWELL: (Teut.) dweller by the wild broom spring
BRUCE: (Old Fr.) from Bruys in Normandy: name of great Scottish hero (Robert)
BRUNO: (Teut.) brown
BRUTUS: (Lat.) stupid
BRYAN: see Brian
BRYCE: (Celt.) rapid, speedy
BRYMER: (Ang.-Sax.) bright
BUDD: (Cymric) rich, victorious
BURDEN: (Teut.) something carried
BURGESS: (Old Eng.) a freeman of the town
BURKE: (Teut.) a stronghold
BURNETT: (Old Fr.) brown
BURTON: (Teut.) a tackle used for rigging ships
BYRLE: (Teut.) a cup-bearer
BYRNE: (Ang.-Sax.) coat of mail

CADELL: (Celt.) battle spirit

CADMAN: (Celt.) strong in battle

CADOC: (Celt.) warlike

CALDWELL: (Teut.) dweller by the cold spring

CALEB: (Heb.) a dog, symbol of fidelity

CALVIN: (Lat.) bold

CAMERON: (Gael.) crooked nose

CAMPBELL: (Gael.) brave man

CARADOC: (Celt.) beloved

CARL, KARL: Teutonic form of Charles

CARLOS: Spanish form of Charles

CARMODY: (Manx) God of arms

CAROLUS: Latin form of Charles

CARROLL: (Celt.) melody

CARVEL: (Manx) a song

CARY: (Teut.) walnut tree

CASEY: (Erse) brook

CASPAR: (Pers.) a horseman

CATO: (Lat.) sagacious

CECIL: (Lat.) blind

CEDA: (Celt.) warlike

CEDRIC: (Celt.) war chief

CEDRON: (Lat.) cedar tree

CHAD: (Celt.) martial

CHAPMAN: (Teut.) merchant

CHARLES: (Teut.) robust, of noble spirit, manly

CHAUNCEY: (Teut.) chancellor

CHENEY: (Lat.) dweller in an oak wood

CHESTER: (Teut.) urban dweller

CHISHOLM: (Teut.) dweller on gravelled land

CHRIS: diminutives of Christian and Christopher

CHRISTIAN: (Gr.) a follower of Christ's teaching

CHRISTOPHER: (Gr.) Christ-bearer (same as French Christophe, Italian Cristoforo, Spanish Cristobal, German Christoph)

CLARENCE: (Lat.) illustrious, famous

38

CLARENDON: (Lat.) famous gentleman

CLARK: (Old Eng.) clergyman, learned man, reader

CLAUD, CLAUDE: (a) English and (b) French forms of Claudius

CLAUDIUS: (Lat.) lame

CLAYTON: (Teut.) from the town on the clay beds

CLEMENT: (Lat.) merciful, mild

CLEON: (Gr.) glorious

CLEVE: (Teut.) a cleft in the land

CLIFFORD: (Teut.) dweller by the ford by the cliff

CLIFTON: dweller at the manor by the cleft rock

CLIVE: origin obscure, but revived from surname of Robert Clive, 18th century, soldier and statesman, also title of poem by Browning

CLYDE: see Clydias

CLYDIAS: (Gr.) glorious

COLA: (Celt.) victorious

COLBERT: (Teut.) cool brightness

COLBURN: (Teut.) dweller by the cold brook

COLERIDGE: (Teut.) dweller by the black ridge

COLIN: (Gr.) victory; (Lat.) dove

COLLINS: (Gr.) victorious

COLVIN: (Teut.) dark friend

COMAN: (Arab.) noble

COMPTON: (Lat.) accumulation

CON: (Celt.) wisdom

CONAL(L): (Gael.) daring all

CONAN: (Celt.) high in wisdom

CONNELL: (Celt.) wise chief

CONNOR: (Teut.) an examiner or inspector

CONRAD: (Teut.) bold and wise counsellor

CONSTANT: English form of Constantine

CONSTANTINE: (Lat.) faithful, resolute

CONWAE: (Celt.) strength, vigour

CONWAY: (Celt.) he who takes a wise course

CORBET: (Old Fr.) raven

CORDELL: (Lat.) a cord

COREY: (Old Eng.) the chosen

CORMAC: doubtful origin, but

probably from (Celt.) son of a chariot

CORNELIUS: (Lat.) horn-like

CORNELL: (Teut.) a dogwood tree

CORRIE: (Gael.) from the mountains

CORWIN: (Teut.) the heart's friend

COSMO: (Gr.) orderly

CRAD(D)OCK: (Celt.) beloved, affectionate

CRAIG: (Gael.) from the mountain crag

CRISPIAN, CRISPIN: (Lat.) curled, having curly hair

CRONAN: (Gr.) a mournful tune

CROSBY: (Teut.) dweller by the crossing

CULVER: (Lat.) a dove

CUTHBERT: (Teut.) brilliant wisdom; (Ang.-Sax.) famous splendour

CYPRIAN: (Lat.) of Cyprus

CYRIL: (Gr.) lord and master, lordly

CYRO: (Pers.) lordly

CYRUS: (Pers.) throne, near the sun

DALE: (Ang.-Sax.) dweller in a vale between hills

DALY: (Old Eng.) a die

DALZIEL: (Gael.) I dare

DAMIAN: (Gr.) taming

DAN: (Heb.) judge, or law giver; also contraction of Daniel

DANA: (Celt.) darling

DANIEL: (Heb.) my judge is God, divine judge

DARAH: (Teut.) bold

DARBY: (Celt.) freeman; (Old Eng.) faithful; also Irish contraction of Diarmid or Diarmaid

DARCY, D'ARCY: (Celt.) dark

DARIAN: (Gr.) daring

DARIUS: (Pers.) preserver; he that informs himself

DARRELL: see Daryl

DARYL: (Ang.-Sax.) darling

DAVID: (Heb.) beloved friend

40

DEAN(E): (Teut.) dweller in the valley

DEARBORN: (Teut.) well-born

DELBERT: (Teut.) nobly bright

DELMAR: (Lat.) man of the sea

DELWIN: (Teut.) godly friend

DENIS, DENNIS: (Gr.) of Dionysius; name frequently used in Ireland, and from which Dennison, Denny, and Dennys have derived

DEREK, DERRICK: (Teut.) people's ruler; Dutch form Diederich, and Old German form Theodoric

DERMOT: (Celt.) father of oaks; an Irish contraction of Diarmid or Diarmaid

DERWOOD: (Teut.) door warden

DESMOND: (Celt.) man of the world

DEVEREAUX: (Old Fr.) dutiful

DEVLIN: (Celt.) heroic; (Gael.) a pilgrim

DEXTER: (Lat.) skilful

DICK: contraction of Richard

DIGBY: (Teut.) a digger

DILLON: (Celt.) faithful

DION: (Gr.) divine

DIGGORY: (Fr.) strayed, lost

DIONYSIUS: (Gr.) see Denis

DOANE: (Celt.) a song

DOLAN: (Celt.) black-haired

DOMINGO: (Span.) Sunday child

DOMINIC: (Lat.) of the Lord, born on a Sunday

DON: (Lat.) master; diminutive of Donald

DONAHUE: (Celt.) dark

DONALD: (Celt.) proud or mighty chief

DONOVAN: (Celt.) dark warrior

DORIAN: (Gr.) a gift

DOUGAL, DOYLE: (Celt.) dark stranger

DOUGLAS: from the surname, or the river

DREW: (Teut.) skilful

DRISCOLL: (Teut.) a thicket of wild roses

DUDLEY: a surname derived from Dudley in Worcestershire and made famous by the Dudley family that rose to power under the Tudors

DUKE: (Lat.) a leader

DUNBAR: (Celt.) dark branch

DUNCAN: (Celt.) dark or brown chief

DUNSTAN: (Teut.) of lofty station; Old Eng. compound of hill and stone

DURAND: (Lat.) enduring, lasting

DURANT: (Lat.) endurance

DURHAM: (Teut.) dweller on a hilly island

DURWOOD: (Teut.) unflinching guard

DWIGHT: origin obscure, perhaps derived from Diot, a diminutive of Dionisia

DYER: (Old Eng.) a colourer of skin and fabrics

EARL, EARLE: (Teut.) of keen intelligence

EARN: (Teut.) an eagle

EBEN: (Heb.) stone; a diminutive of Ebenezer

EBENEZER: (Heb.) stone of help

EBER: (Heb.) one that passes

EBERARD: (Teut.) strong and hardy

ED: (Teut.) wealth; (Heb.) a witness; also a diminutive of Edward

EDAN: (Celt.) fire

EDDY: (Scan.) unresting

EDEL: (Teut.) noble

EDGAR: (Teut.) rich spear; (Ang.-Sax.) dart

EDMOND, EDMUND: (Teut.) rich protection; (Ang.-Sax.) defender of property

EDRED: (Teut.) rich counsel

EDRIC: (Teut.) rich ruler

EDWARD: (Teut.) rich ward, or guardian of property

EDWIN: (Teut.) rich friend

EGAN: (Gael.) strong handed

EGBERT: (Teut.) eminently bright; (Ang.-Sax.) skilled with the sword

ELEAZAR: (Heb.) God helped

ELBERT: same as Albert

ELDO: (Gr.) a wish

ELDON: (Lat.) the gift

ELDRED: (Teut.) mature counsellor

ELDWIN: (Teut.) old friend

ELI: (Heb.) elevation; the high

ELGIN: (Gael.) earldom of the Bruces of Scotland

ELIA: (Heb.) God's own

ELIAS: (Lat.) cheerful

ELIOT, ELLIOT, ELLIOTT: (Heb.) God's own given one

ELISHA: (Heb.) God is generous, God is my salvation

ELKAN: (Heb.) God created

ELLERY: modern usage

ELLIS: English variant of Elisha

ELMER: (Ang.-Sax.) noble

ELMO: (Gr.) amiable

ELMORE: (Teut.) the greater

ELON: (Heb.) the sturdy oak

ELROY: (Lat.) regal

ELVAN: (Teut.) quick willed

ELWIN, ELWYN: Godly friend

EMANUEL, EMMANUEL: (Heb.) God (is) with us

EMERIA: (Teut.) industrious worker

EMERY: (Teut.) powerful; (Ang.-Sax.) strong, rich

EMIL: (Teut.) industrious

EMRYS: a Welsh name derived from Ambrose

ENOCH: (Heb.) the dedicated

ENSLEY: (Celt.) a watchword

EOGHAN: (Celt.) young warrior

EPHRAIM: (Heb.) fruitful

ERASMUS: (Gr.) the desired

ERASTUS: (Gr.) amiable

ERIC: (Teut.) kingly; (Ang.-Sax.) brave; powerful

ERLON: (Teut.) elfish

ERMOS: (Teut.) popular

ERNEST: (Teut.) of serious purpose

ERNST: German form of Ernest

ERROL: (Lat.) wandering

ERVAND: (Scan.) sea warrior

ERWIN: (Teut.) friend

ESAU: (Heb.) he that finishes; also, rough, hairy

ESBERN: (Teut.) divine leader

ESDRAS: (Heb.) a rising light

ESMOND: (Teut.) protected by the gods

ESTEVAN: (Basque-Gr.) a crown

ETHAN: (Heb.) firmness

ETHELBERT: (Ang.-Sax.) noble and bright

ETHELRED: (Ang.-Sax.) noble strength, noble counsel

EUCLID: (Gr.) true glory

EUCRATES: (Gr.) good tempered

EUGENE: (Gr.) well-born, noble

EUSEBIUS: (Gr.) pious, God-fearing

EUSTACE: (Gr.) fruitful harvest, steadfast

EVAN: (Celt.) young warrior

EVAR: (Heb.) life

EVERARD: (Teut.) ever courageous, strong as a boar

EVERETT: (Teut.) courageous

EWALD: (Teut.) always powerful

EWAN, EWEN: (Celt.) warrior

EWART: (Teut.) brave

EYMER: (Teut.) royal toiler

EZEKIEL: (Heb.) may God strengthen

EZRA: (Heb.) help, the helpful

FABIAN: (Lat.) thought to have derived from "faba", a bean, therefore a bean-grower. (Other authorities give this as dilatory.)

FAGAN: (Celt.) small voice

FAIRCHILD: (Teut.) blond child

FAIRFAX: (Teut.) fair-haired

FALKNER: (Teut.) trainer of hawks

FANE: (Teut.) joyful

FARLEY: (Teut.) unexpected

FARNHAM: (Teut.) village in the ferns

FARQUHAR: (Gael.) friendly man

FARREL: (Arab.) a bearer of burdens

FELIX: (Lat.) happy

FEODORE: a variant of Theodore

FERDINAND: (Teut.) venturing; brave

FERGUS: (Celt.) man of strength

FERRIS: (Lat.) man of iron

FESTUS: (Lat.) the joyful

FILIBERT: (Teut.) of flashing will

FILMER: (Teut.) most famous

FINGAL: (Celt.) mythical Irish hero, white stranger

FINLEY: (Gael.) sunbeam

FLAVIAN: (Lat.) yellow-haired

FLETCHER: (Teut.) arrow maker

FORD: (Teut.) crossing or passing

FRANCIS: (Teut.) free

FRANK: an English contraction of Francis

FRANKLIN, FRANKLYN: (Teut.) a freeman

FRAYNE: (Teut.) the ash tree

FRED: an English contraction of Frederick

FREDERICK: (Teut.) peace ruler

FREEMAN: (Ang.-Sax.) not a slave

FREWEN: (Ang.-Sax.) free friend

FRITZ: (Teut.) peaceful ruler

GABRIEL: (Heb.) strong man of God

GALAHAD: (Celt.) valorous; name of spotless knight who succeeded in his quest of the Holy Grail

GALE: (Scan.) a wind; (Danish) a crow

GALPIN: (Old Fr.) a runner

GARCIA: (Teut.) a warrior

GARNER, GARNIER: (Teut.) protecting warrior

GARNET, GARRET: (Teut.) strong with the spear

GARRICK: (Teut.) warrior king

GARRY: see Garvey

GARTH: (Ang.-Sax.) form of gardener

GARVEY: (Teut.) spear-bearer

GASPARD: (Pers.) treasure master

GASTON: (Teut.) hospitable; (Span.) beautiful town

GAVIN: (Celt.) hawk of battle

GAYLE: (Teut.) a jailor

GAWAIN: Welsh form of Gavin

GAYLORD: (Teut.) merry lord

GAYNOR: (Celt.) fair head

GEBHARD: (Teut.) determined giver

GENE: a contraction of Eugene

GEOFFREY: (Teut.-Fr.) God's peace

GEORGE: (Gr.) tiller of the soil

GERAINT: (Teut.) unerring spear

GERALD: (Teut.) strong with a spear

GERARD: English form of Gerald

GERHARD: German form of Gerard

GERRY: diminutive of Gerald and Gerard

GERVAISE: (Teut.) alert warrior

GIDEON: (Heb.) a hewer

GIFFORD: (Teut.) a passing

GILBERT: (Teut.) bright pledge

GILCHRIST: (Celt.) servant of Christ

GILES: (Gr.) a shield, or shield-bearer; (Lat.) a young goat

GILLIAN: (Celt.) servant of the saints

GILMAN: (Teut.) big man

GILMORE, GILMOUR: (Teut.) big servant; (Celt.) a servant of Mary

GLADE: (Old Eng.) shining

GLADSTONE: (Ang.-Sax.) polished rock

GLADWIN: (Teut.) merry friend

GLEN: (Teut.) a dale

GLOVER: (Teut.) one who makes or sells gloves

GLYNN: (Teut.) from the glen

GODDARD: (Teut.) divinely resolute, pious

GODFREY: (Teut.) peace of God

GODRIC: (Teut.) friend of God

GODWIN: (Ang.-Sax.) brave in war

GORDON: (Teut.) dweller at the triangular hill estate

GORHAM: (Old Eng.) dweller at the mud house

GRAHAM: (Teut.) dweller in the grey manor; stern

GRANT: (Old Eng.) a promise

GRANTHAM: (Old Eng.) a home acquired by deed

GRASHAM, GRESHAM; (Teut.) dweller on the grassland

GREGORY: (Gr.) watchful

GRIFFITH: (Lat.) ruddy

GROSVENOR: (Old Fr.) great hunter

GROVER: (Teut.) one who dwells among the trees

GUIDO: (Teut.) a guide

GUILFORD: (Teut.) William's ford

GUILLYM: Welsh form of William

GUNTHAR: (Teut.) warrior, bold

GURTH: (Teut.) bonded

GUSTAV(E), GUSTAVUS: (Teut.) Goth's staff

GUY: (Celt.) sensible; (Fr.) guide, leader

GWYN: (Cymric) a hunter

HADLEY: (Teut.) landholder

HAGBERT: (Teut.) skilful

HAIMA: (Sans.) made of gold

HAINES: (Cymric) one who helps himself

HAL: (Ang.-Sax.) healthy; contraction of Henry, and of Harold

HALBERT: see Albert

HALI: (Teut.) in sound health

HALL: (Teut.) stone or rock; a manor house

HALLETT: (Teut.) dweller at the little manor

HALLAM: (Teut.) a threshold

HAMAL: (Turkish) a carrier

HAMAN: (Heb.) magnificent

HAMISH: Gaelic form of James

HAMLYN: (Teut.) home lover

HAMO: (Teut.) home

HANNIBAL: (Phoenician) grace of the supreme being;

(Egypt.) favoured of Baal

HANS: a German form of John

HARALD: a Danish form of Harold

HARDING: (Teut.) resolute

HARDWIN: (Teut.) hard friend

HARLEY: (Teut.) dear hunter

HAROLD: (Teut.) a compound of "here" and "weald" — army and power; (Ang.-Sax.) a champion, a general

HARPER: (Teut.) harp player

HARRISON: modern usage

HARRY: English form of Henry

HART: (Teut.) the stag

HARTLEY: (Teut.) dweller by the lea of the stags

HARVEY: (Celt.) progressive

HASAKA: (Sans.) a jester

HASTINGS: (Teut.) swift

HAVELOCK: (Lat.) tent

HAYDEN: (Teut.) dweller on a ledged hill

HAYES: modern usage

HAYMON: an Old English variant of Hamo

HAYWARD: (Teut.) guard of the ledge

HAYWOOD: (Teut.) the wood within the ledge

HEATH: (Teut.) a high plain

HECTOR: (Gr.) an anchor, thought to have originally meant holding fast

HEDLEY: (Teut.) the upper meadow

HEINRICH: a German form of Henry

HELGA: a Norse name meaning holy

HENLY: (Teut.) home lover

HENRY: (Teut.) ruler of the home

HERBERT: (Teut.) bright warrior; (Ang.-Sax.) army hero

HER(R)IOT: obsolete diminutive of Henry

HERMAN: (Teut.) army or war man

HERRICK: (Teut.) army commander

HEW: (Celt.) mind, a variant of Hugh

HEYWARD: (Teut.) dweller by the dark forest

HEZEKIAH: (Heb.) God is strength

HILARY: (Lat.) cheerful

HIRAM: (Heb.) nobly born

HOBART: a variant of Hubert

48

HODGE: (Teut.) famous swordsman

HOGAN: (Dutch) eminent

HORACE, HORATIO: (Lat.) light of the sun, worthy

HOWARD: (Teut.) hedge guard

HOWELL: (Wel.) eminent

HUBBARD: (Teut.) intellectual

HUBERT: (Teut.) bright

HUGH: (Teut.) intellectual

HUGO: a form of Hugh

HUMBERT: (Teut.) bright giant

HUMPHREY: (Ang.-Sax.) protector of the home

HUNTER: (Teut.) huntsman

HURLEY: Irish game of hockey

HUYA: (N.A. Ind.) fighting eagle

HYLAND: (Teut.) highlander

HYMAN: (Teut.) high dweller

IA(I)N: see John

IAN: (Heb.) God's grace

IBALD: (Teut.) princely archer

ICABOD: (Heb.) departed glory

IGNATIUS: (Lat.) ardent: (Gr.) the kindled flame

ILBERT: (Teut.) strife

ILLARIS: (Gr.) merry

ILLAH: (Heb.) a tree

IMALA: (N.A. Ind.) a disciplinarian

IMMANUEL: see Emanuel

IMO: (Gr.) beloved

INGOMA: (Teut.) of Ing's fame

INGRAM: (Teut.) raven

INIGO: origin obscure; name of a bishop of Antioch, martyred between A.D. 104 and 117; also name of English architect, Inigo Jones

INNIS: (Teut.) sheltered valley

IRA: (Heb.) descendant; (Aramaic) the stallion

IRAM: (Heb.) citizen

IRWIN: modern usage

IRVING: modern usage

ISAAC: (Heb.) laughter

ISAIAH: (Heb.) the Lord is his salvation

ISAS: (Jap.) meritorious

ISHI: (Heb.) husband

ISHMAEL: (Heb.) God heareth

ISIDORE: (Gr.) gift of Isis

ISRAEL: (Heb.) authorities give this as both "may God prevail" and "soldier of God"

IVAN: Russian form of John

IVER: (Old Scan.) military archer

IVOR: (Teut.) bow bearer

IXARA: (Sans.) master, prince

IZOD: (Celt.) fair

JABEZ: (Heb.) obscure meaning: some authorities give it as sorrow

JACK: an English contraction of John; 19th century authority stated that, contrary to belief at the time, there was no confirmation of the theory that Jack or Jakke was ever used to represent Jacques or James

JACOB: (Heb.) a supplanter

JACQUES: French form of James

JADA: (Sans.) frigid

JAMES: from Jacobus: English form of Jacob

JAN: a dialectal form of John

JAPHET(H): (Heb.) may he expand

JARED: (Gr.) rose

JARVIS: (Old Eng.) a driver

JASON: (Gr.) healer

JASPER: (Pers.) treasure seeker

JAY: (Teut.) gay

JEFFERSON: (Teut.) son of peace

JEFFREY: see Geoffrey

JEHU: (Heb.) Jehovah is he

JEPHTHAH: (Heb.) God sets free

JEREMIAH, JEREMY: (Heb.) exalted of God

JERMYN: (Teut.) bright

JEROME: (Gr.) sacred name

JERRY: diminutives of Gerald, Gerard, and Jeremy

JERVIS: (Teut.) alert warrior (another form of Gervaise)

JERVOISE: a variant of Jervis and Gervaise

JERWAIS: (Teut.) armed for battle

JESSE: (Heb.) wealthy

JESUS: (Heb.) saviour, healing

JETHRO: (Heb.) abundance

JEVON: Welsh form of Evan

JIM: an English contraction of James

JIVANTA: (Sans.) long lived

JIVIN: (Sans.) vivifying

JOAB: (Heb.) God (Jehovah) is (his) father

JOACHIM: (Heb.) may Jehovah exalt

JOB: (Heb.) persecuted

JOCELIN: (Lat.) sportive

JOCK: see Jacob; also a Scottish form of John

JODA: (Lat.) playful

JOE: an English contraction of Joseph

JOEL: (Heb.) Jehovah is God

JOHN: (Heb.) Jehovah has favoured, the Lord graciously giveth

JOLON: (N.A. Ind.) valley of the dead oaks

JONAH, JONAS: (Heb.) a dove

JONATHAN: (Heb.) the Lord's gift

JORAH: (Heb.) autumn rain

JORDAN: (Heb.) flowing down, descendant

JOSEPH: (Heb.) may Jehovah add

JOSHUA: (Heb.) the Lord is salvation; Jehovah is generous

JOSIAH: (Heb.) may Jehovah heal

JOSIAS: a Greek form of Josiah

JOTHAM: (Heb.) Jehovah is perfect

JOVITA: (Teut.) little dove

JOYCE: (Lat.) merry; used for both men and women

JUAN: a Spanish form of John

JUDAH: (Heb.) praised

JULES: variant of Julius

JULIAN: variant of Julius

JULIUS: (Lat.) soft-haired, or downy-bearded

JUSTIN: see Justus

JUSTUS: (Lat.) just

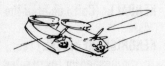

51

KAI: (Pers.) king

KALEVA: (Finn.) a hero

KANE: (Lat.) exacted tribute

KARL: (Teut.) a man; German form of Charles

KASPAR: (Pers.) treasure master

KAY: (Gr.) rejoicing

KEANE: (Celt.) great, vast

KEARNEY: (Celt.) a soldier

KEENAN: (Celt.) sharp

KEIRA: (Teut.) ever regal

KEITH: (Gael.) the wind

KELLY: (Celt.) a warrior

KELVIN: see Kelwin

KELWIN: (Teut.-Celt.) warrior friend

KEMBLE: (Ang.-Sax.) royally bold

KENDALL: (Celt.) chief of the dale

KENDRICK, KENRICK: (Teut.) distinguished (or royal) ruler

KENELM: (Celt.) beloved chief

KENNA: (Celt.) quick love

KENNEDY: (Celt.) chief of the clan

KENNETH: (Gael.) leader

KENNY: diminutive of Kenneth

KENT: (Celt.) chief

KENWARD: (Teut.) keen guardian

KENWOOD: (Celt.) wooded dell

KERR: (Celt.) a meadow

KERRIN, KERRYN: variants of Kieren

KERRY: (Ang.-Sax.) captain

KERSEY: (Old Eng.) homely

KERWIN: (Teut.) loving friend

KERWOOD: (Gael.) dweller at the wood by the meadow

KESTER: a variant of Christopher

KETURAH: (Heb.) fragrance

KEVIN: (Celt.) comely; (Old Irish) comely birth

KIEREN: (Celt.) black

KILBURN: (Teut.) keen guardian

KIM: (Ang.-Sax.) chief

KIMBALL: modern usage

KING: (Teut.) chief

KINGSLEY: (Teut.) dweller in the royal meadow

KINGSTON: (Teut.) dweller at the royal residence

KINMAN: (Ang.-Sax.) man of royal blood

KIRLEY: (Arab.) a waterskin

KIRK: (Gael.) a house of worship

KIRKHAM: (Teut.) dweller at the church manor

KIRKLAND: (Teut.) dweller on church land

KIRKWOOD: (Teut.) dweller in the wood by the church

KIT: a contraction of Christopher

KNOWLES: (Teut.) a grassy slope in the forest

KONRAD: see Conrad

KURTZ: (Teut.) short, laconic in speech

KYLE: (Gael.) a channel or firth

KYRLE: modern usage

L

LACHLAN: (Celt.) probably derived from "Laochail", meaning warlike, other references give this as by the sea, or inlet

LAMBERT: (Teut.) compound of two words meaning land and bright; other authorities give this as both his country's glory, and illustrious with landed possessions

LANCE: abbreviation of Lancelot

LANCELOT: (Ital.) a little lance; (Lat.) he who serves

LANDERS: (Teut.) son of a rural dweller

LANDIS: (Teut.) nature

LANDON: (Teut.) dweller on the mill

LANDOR: (Teut.) country dweller

LANDRY: (Teut.) manor lord

LANE: (Teut.) a passage-way

LANGDON: (Teut.) dweller at the long hill

LANGFORD: (Teut.) dweller at the lord ford

LANGLEY: (Teut.) dweller at the long meadow

LANN: (Celt.) a sward

LARKIN: (Lat.) laurel

LARRY: a contraction of Laurence

LARS: (Etruscan) lord

LATIMER: (Teut.) an interpreter

LAUNCELOT: a variant of Lancelot

LAURENCE, LAWRENCE: (Lat.) laurel; crowned with laurel

LAURIE: a contraction of Laurence or Lawrence

LAVERNE: (Lat.) flourishing

LAWLOR: (Teut.) law lord

LEA: (Lat.) a meadow

LEAL: (Lat.) loyal

LEALAND: (Teut.) meadowland

LEANDER: (Gr.) lion-like

LEGER: (Teut.) the people's defending spear

LEHMAN: (Teut.) a feudal tenant

LEIGH: variant of Lea

LEIGHTON: (Teut.) dweller in a garden of herbs

LEMUEL: (Heb.) God's own

LENNOX: see Lenox

LENOX: (Gael.) chieftain

LENUS: (Lat.) mild

LEO: (Lat.-Gr.) lion

LEON: (Gr.) of lion nature

LEONARD: (Gr.) strong and brave as a lion

LEONIDAS: (Gr.) lion-like

LEOPOLD: (Teut.) bold for the people

LESLIE: (Teut.) one who leases

LESTER: (Ang.-Sax.) shining

LEVANDER: (Old Fr.) an easterly wind blowing off the Mediterranean

LEVI: (Arab.) priest; (Heb.) a concord

LEWIS: (Teut.) famous warrior; a name popular in Wales

LINDEN: (Teut.) gentle

LINDHURST: (Teut.) tranquil wood

LINDLEY: (Teut.) dweller in

the tranquil meadow

LINDSAY: see Lindsey

LINDSEY: (Teut.) of gentle speech

LIONEL: (Lat.) young lion

LISLE: (Lat.) isle (from the)

LLEWELLYN: (Celt.) lightning; (Cymrjc) the lighting sovereign

LLOYD: (Celt.) grey

LLYN: (Cymric) by the sea

LOCHINVAR: (Gael.) origin obscure, but probably some Scottish lake

LOGAN: (Old Eng.) a rocking stone

LOK: (Chin.) happiness

LOMBARD: (Ang.-Sax.) a long beard

LOREDO: (Lat.) learned

LORENZO: see Laurence

LORIMER: (Lat.) maker of bridles

LORING: (Lat.) instructive

LORNE: (Gael.) bereft, forlorn

LORY: (Malayan) a species of parrot

LOT: (Heb.) a covering veil; (Celt.) lion

LOTHARIO: (Teut.) famous warrior

LOUIS: a French form of Lewis

LOVEL: (Teut.) a young wolf

LOVELACE: (Old Eng.) a love token

LOVELL: (Teut.) wolf

LOVICK: (Ang.-Sax.) beloved ruler

LOWELL: (Teut.) dweller by the low spring

LOY: (Chin.) open

LUBIN: (Teut.) a beloved friend

LUCAS: see Lucian

LUCIAN: (Lat.) light

LUCIEN: see Lucian

LUCIUS: (Lat.) light bringer

LUDLOW: (Teut.) lowly man

LUDWIG: (Teut.) famous warrior

LUIS: Spanish form of Louis

LUTHER: (Gr.) illustrious warrior

LYLE: English dialectical contraction of little; (Teut.) an island

LYN: (Ang.-Sax.) a torrent or cascade

LYNDELL: (Teut.) dweller by the cascade in the dell

LYNDON: (Teut.) dweller on a hill beside the castle

LYULF: (Scan.) fiery wolf

MAC: (Gael.) son of

MACAIRE: (Gr.) happy

MADDOX: (Cymric) force

MAGAN: (Teut.) power

MAGNUS: (Lat.) great

MALACHI: (Heb.) God's messenger

MALCOLM: (Gael.) servant or disciple of Colomb

MANCHU: (Chin.) pure

MANDEL: (Old Fr.) a mantle

MANFRED: (Teut.) man of peace

MANOC: (Heb.) great

MANUEL: see Emmanuel

MARC: (Heb.) bitter

MARCEL: (Lat.) of warlike qualities

MARCIUS: (Lat.) martial

MARCUS: see Marcius

MARK: English form of Marcius

MARMADUKE: (Celt.) leader at sea: (Ang.-Sax.) a great noble

MARMION: (Gael.) sparkling fame

MARTEN: (Lat.) bearer of the sable

MARTIN: see Marcius

MASON: (Teut.) a worker in stone

MAT(T): an abbreviation of Matthew and Matthias

MATTHEW, MATTHIAS: (Heb.) gift of Jehovah

MAURICE: (Lat.) a Moor, Moorish

MAXIM: (Lat.) a premise, serving as a rule or guide

MAXIMILIAN: (Lat.) the greatest Emilius (Aemilianus); often abbreviated to Max

MAXWELL: (Teut.) dweller by the big spring; some authorities give this as a variant of Maximilian

MAYER: (Old Eng.) one who goes a-maying

MAYNARD: (Teut.) hardy strength, might

MAYNE: (Teut.) mighty

MAYO: (Ang.-Sax.) kinsman

MEADE: (Teut.) a strong draught

MELBOURNE: (Lat.) favourable destiny

MELCHIOR: (Heb.) King of Light

MELDON: (Lat.) favourable or pleasant gift

MELFORD: (Gr.) the ford by the mill

MELLIS: (Celt.) disciple of Jesus

MELVA: (Celt.) chief

MELVILLE: (Celt.) chief of the people

MELVIN: (Celt.) chief, a variant of Melva

MEREDITH: (Celt.) coastguard, sea protector

MERGUS: (Lat.) a diver

MERIVALE: modern usage

MERLE: (Teut.) a blackbird

MERLIN: (Celt.) a hill by the sea

MERRILL: (Teut.) famous

MERVIN, MERVYN: (Celt.) raven of the sea

METHUSELAH: (Heb.) man of; used in 16th-18th centuries

METIS: (Gr.) a counsellor

MEYER: (Teut.) steward

MACAH: (Heb.) one who is like Jehovah

MICHAEL: (Heb.) one who is like the Lord, godly

MICK, MIKE: contractions of Michael

MILES: (Lat.) a soldier

MILFORD: (Teut.) dweller by the mill by the ford

MILTON: (Teut.) mill town

MILWARD: (Teut.) mill keeper

MITCHELL: (Teut.) a small loaf of bread

MONACO: (Lat.) solitary

MONROE: (Celt.) dweller by the red morass: derived from Mont Roe, a river on the river Roe in Ireland

MONTAGUE: (Old Eng.) from "Mont Aigu"

MONTE: (Lat.) a mountain

MONTGOMERY: (Lat.) huntsman

MONTROSE: (Lat.-Eng.) rose of the mountain

MORAG: (Gael.) the sun

MORAY: (Celt.) original form of Murray

MORELAND: (Teut.) dweller by the moorland

MORGAN: (Teut.) sea-born, seaman

MORICE: a variant of Maurice

MORLEY: (Teut.) dweller by the meadow

MORRIS: (Lat.) a moor

MORTIMER: (Celt.) sea warrior

MORVEN: (Celt.) seaman

MOSES: (Egypt.) drawn out of the water; (Gr.) drawn from the water; (Heb.) the rescued servant of God

MUNGO: (Gael.) amiable

MUNROE: modern usage; see Monroe

MURDOCH, MURDOCK: (Gael.) sea man

MURPHY: (Celt.) sea warrior

MURRAY: (Celt.) a seaman

MYLES: a variant of Miles or Mills

MYRON: (Gr.) fragrant

NADA: (Sans.) thunder, aware

NAHUM: (Heb.) consoling

NALA: (Sans.) legendary king

NAMAN: (Sans.) a name

NAPIER: (Gr.) of the new city

NAT: abbreviations of Nathan, Nathanael and Nathaniel

NATHANAEL, NATHANIEL: (Heb.) God has given

NEAL, NEIL: (Celt.) chief, champion; variants of Nigel

NED: see Edward

NEHEMIAH: (Heb.) comfort of Jehovah

NEILL: see Neal

NERO: (Lat.) strong, stern

NESTOR: (Gr.) he who remembers

NEVAN: (Gr.) a name

NEVILLE: (Lat.) of the new city

NICHOLAS, NICOLAS: (Gr.) victor of the people

NICK, NICKY: contractions of Nicholas, Nicolas

NIGEL: origin obscure, but probably of Irish origin; thought to mean dark

NIMROD: (Heb.) fiery red

NOAH: (Heb.) long rest, consolation

NOEL: (Old Eng.) the nativity; born on Christmas Day

NORBERT: (Teut.) divine brightness

NORMAN: (Old Eng.) a man from the north; (Scan.) divine man

NORRIS: (Teut.) north king

NORUA: (Teut.) divine strength

NORVEL: (Fr.) from the northern city

NOWELL: (Teut.) variant of Noel

OBADIAH: (Heb.) serving the Lord

OCTAVIUS, OCTAVUS: (Lat.) eighth son

ODIC: (Gr.) a song or ode

ODO: (Teut.) rich

OLAF: (Teut.) ancestor's relic; a name adopted by Swedish kings

OLIVER: (Lat.) the olive or olive tree, suggesting peace

ORBAN: (Lat.) citizen

ORMOND: (Teut.) famous protector

ORSINO: (Lat.) bear-like, superior qualities

ORSON: a variant of Orsino

OSBERT: (Teut.) brightness of a god

OSBORN: (Teut.) sacred bear; (Old Eng.) godly bear

OSCAR: (Celt.) bounding warrior

OSMOND: (Teut.) protected by God

OSWALD: (Teut.) divine power

OTTO: (Teut.) rich, variant of Odo

OWEN: (Celt.) warrior; (Lat.) well born

P

PABLO: (Span.) little

PADDY: a contraction of Patrick

PALMER: (Middle Eng.) palm-bearer, pilgrim to the Holy Land

PAOLO: (Lat.) a little stone

PARKER: (Teut.) keeper of a park

PARRY: (Lat.) equality

PASCAL: (Heb.) deliverance; Easter child, or Passover child

PASCOE: an English variant of Pascal

PAT: a contraction of Patrick

PATRICK: (Lat.) patrician, nobleman

PAUL: (Lat.) small, an English form of Paulus

PAULUS: (Lat.) small

PAYNE: (Lat.) rustic

PEDRO: a Spanish form of Peter

PERCIVAL: (Fr.) pierce the valley; (Gr.) courteous

PERCY: a diminutive of Percival

PEREGRINE: (Lat.) stranger, pilgrim traveller

PETER: (Lat.-Gr.) a rock

PHELIM: (Celt.) good

PHILEMON: (Gr.) kiss, loving

PHILIP: (Gr.) a lover of horses

PHINEAS: (Heb.) mouth of brass

PIERCE: modern usage

PIERRE: French form of Peter

PIERS: an early English form of Peter

PYTHIAS: (Gr.) the inquiring

QUENTIN: (Lat.) fifth, the fifth son

QUERON: (Celt.) black or dark

QUILLER: (Teut.) a fledgling

QUINTON: a variant of Quentin

QUONG: (Chin.) bright

RADCLIFFE: (Teut.) red cliff

RADFORD: dweller by the swift water ford

RAFAEL: see Raphael

RALPH: from Old Eng. word Raedwulf, a compound of counsel and wolf, which became Radulf and then Ralf: (Teut.) house wolf; also probably a contraction of Randolf

RAMON: (Teut.) protecting judge

RAMSAY, RAMSEY: (Teut.) the strong

RANA: (Sans.) prince

RANDAL: variant of Randolf

RANDOLF, RANDOLPH: (Teut.) house wolf

RAPHAEL: (Heb.) God has healed

RAY: abbreviation of Raymond

RAYMOND: (Teut.) wise or good protector

RAYNOR: (Teut.) wise or discreet warrior

REDMOND: (Teut.) protecting counsellor

REGINALD: see Reynold

REUBEN: (Heb.) renewer; a child that has taken the place of one that has died

REX: (Lat.) king

REYBURN: (Teut.) a flaming way

REYNOLD: (Lat.-Teut.) regal judgment, power might

RHYS: (Celt.) a chief

RICHARD: (Teut.) harsh king, an Old Eng. compound of ruler and hard

RICHMOND: (Teut.) the protecting ruler

ROBERT: (Teut.) bright flame

ROBIN: Scottish diminutive of Robert

RODERIC, RODERICK: (Teut.) rich in fame

RODGER: (Teut.) praise

RODNEY: (Teut.) famous

ROGER: see Rodger

RODOLPH: (Teut.) hero, wolf

ROLAND: (Teut.) fame of the land

ROLLO: see Rodolph

RONALD: (Teut.) powerful counsel; Scottish equivalent of Ronald and Reginald

RORY: (Celt.) red

ROSS: (Teut.) a horse

ROWLAND: see Roland

ROYCE, ROYSTON: (Teut.) royal

RUDOLPH: see Rodolph

RUFUS: (Lat.) red, red-haired

RUPERT: same as Robert

RUSSELL: (Teut.) the fox

SABAS: (Heb.) rest

SALVADOR: (Lat.) saviour

SAMSON, SAMPSON: (Heb.) splendid sun

SAMUEL: (Heb.) heard of God, in the name of God

SANCHO: (Lat.) holy

SAUL: (Heb.) longed for, asked of God

SCOTT: modern usage

SEAFORTH: (Teut.) peaceful conqueror

SEBASTIAN: (Gr.) venerable

SEPTIMUS: (Lat.) the seventh child

SERLO: (Teut.) armour

SETH: (Heb.) the appointed

SEXTUS: (Lat.) the sixth child

SEYMOUR: (Teut.) the sower

SHANE: an Irish form of John

SHANAHAN: (Celt.) sagacious

SHAMUS: Irish form of James

SHAWN: (Heb.) grace of the Lord

SHEEAN: (Celt.) courteous

SHELDON: (Teut.) shield bearer

SHERIDAN: (Erse) wild man

SHOLTO: (Celt.) sower

SID: (Teut.) conqueror

SILAS: (Lat.) of the forest; god of trees

SILVESTER: (Lat.) growing in a wood, forest dweller

SIMON: a form of Simeon
SOLOMON: (Heb.) man of peace
SPENCER: (Old Eng.) a dispenser (of provisions)
STACY: (Lat.) stable dependable
STANISLAUS: (Slav.) camp glory
STANLEY: (Teut.) a form of Stanislaus
STATON: (Teut.) of the stone dwelling
STEPHEN: (Gr.) a crown
STERLING: (Teut.) true
STEWART, STUART: (Teut.) an administrator
SWAIN: (Teut.) a youth in service
SYDNEY: (Teut.) of St Denys
SYLVESTER: see Silvester

TABOR: (Turkish) a fortified encampment

TALBOT: (Old Eng.) name of original stock of blood-hounds, used in heraldic signs
TATE: (N.A. Ind.) windy, a great talker
TAYLOR: (Teut.) a cutter of cloth
TEAGUE: (Celt.) poet
TED, TEDDY: contractions of Edward and Theodore
TERENCE: (Lat.) tender
TERRY: (Teut.) well-respected ruler, also a contraction of Terence
THADDEUS: (Syriac) wise; (Aramaic) praise
THEODORE: (Gr.) divine gift
THEOPHILUS: (Gr.) loved of God
THOMAS: (Aramaic-Heb.) twin
THOROLD: (Scan.) having power from Thor
THURLOW: (Teut.) Thor's sport; (Celt.) a low tower
THURSTAN, THURSTON: (Teut.) Thor's jewel; (Danish) stone
TIM: see Timothy
TIMOTHY: Greek compound

63

of honour, respect and a god; (Heb.) God-fearing

TOBIAH, TOBIAS: (Heb.) the Lord is good

TOM: an English contraction of Thomas

TONY: a contraction of Anthony and Antony

TOOLE: (Celt.) lordly

TORQUIL: (Nor.) from the god, Thor

TRACY, TRACEY: (Old Eng.) a pathway

TRAFFORD: (Lat.-Teut.) dweller beyond the ford

TRAVERS: (Old Fr.) athwart

TREVOR: (Celt.) discreet

TRISTRAM: (Celt.) tumult; (Lat.) grave, sorrowful

UDO: (Lat.) humid

ULRICK: (Teut.) noble ruler

UNO: (Lat.) the One, a name meaning perfection

ULYSSES: (Gr.) the hater

URBAN: (Lat.) of the town

URIAH: (Heb.) light of the Lord

URLWIN: (Teut.) noble friend

VAL: see Valentine

VALENTINE: (Lat.) strong, healthy

VALERY: (Teut.) fierce ruler

VAN: (Dutch) noble descent

VAUGHAN: (Celt.) little

VERNON: (Lat.) flourishing

VICTOR: (Lat.) conqueror

VINCENT: (Lat.) conquering

VIVIAN: (Lat.) lively

VLADIMIR: (Slav.) the glory of ruling princes

VYVIAN, VYVYAN: variants of Vivian

WADE: (Dutch) a meadow

WALDEMAR: (Teut.) celebrated power

WALDEN: (Teut.) mighty

WALDO: see Walden

WALLACE: (Lat.) foreigner

WALTER: (Teut.) powerful

WARD: (Teut.) one who keeps guard

WARNER: (Old Fr.) to guard; (Teut.) protecting warrior

WARREN: (Teut.) a park

WARWICK: (Teut.) camp

WAYNE: (Teut.) an ancient wagon

WENDELL: (Teut.) a wanderer

WESLEY: see Westley

WESTLEY: (Ang.-Sax.) of the west meadow

WILBUR: (Teut.) bright resolve

WILFRED, WILFRID: (Teut.) resolute peace

WILL: a contraction of William

WILLIAM: derived from old German compound of will and helmet; resolute helmet, defender

WILMER: (Teut.) of famous resolution

WILMOT: (Teut.) resolute

WINSTON: (Teut.) a dweller in a friendly town

XAVIER: (Arab.) bright

XENEK: (Gr.) a stranger

XENOS: (Gr.) strange

YARDLEY: (Teut.) dweller in the meadow pastures

YEMON: (Jap.) guarding the gate
YVE, YVES: French derivative of Ivo
YVON: (Teut.) archer
YWAIN: (Celt.) young warrior

ZABROS: (Gr.) glutton
ZACHARIAS, ZACHARY: (Heb.) remembered of Jehovah

ZADOK: (Heb.) the just
ZARAB: (Sudan) protection against enemies
ZEDEKIAH: (Heb.) righteousness of Jehovah
ZEL: (Pers.) cymbal
ZELOS: (Gr.) emulation
ZENOS: (Gr.) Jupiter's gift
ZERAH: (Heb.) a rising light
ZIVAN: (Slav.) lively
ZURIAL: (Heb.) God is my rock

GIRLS

ACIMA: (Heb.) the Lord will judge

ADAH: (Heb.) ornament

ADERYN: (Wel.) bird

ADIEL: (Heb.) ornament of the Lord

AELWEN: (Wel.) fair brow

AENEA: (Heb.) praiseworthy

AERONA: (Wel.) like a berry

AERONWEN: (Wel.) fair berry

AFRA: (Teut.) peaceful ruler; (Heb.) dust

AGEE: (Heb.) one who flees

AGRIPPINA: (Lat.) born feet foremost

AISLINN: (Celt.) dream, vision

ALA: (Teut.) holy

ALANA: (Celt.) my child

ALBERTINA: (Ang.-Sax.) bright or illustrious; a feminine form of Albert

ALBINA, ALBINIA: (Lat.) white

ALCINA: (Gr.) sea-maiden

ALDIS: (Old Eng.) from the old house

ALDORA: (Gr.) winged gift

ALETHA: (Gr.) truth

ALETTA: (Lat.) winged, little wing

ALEXIA: (Teut.) a German form of Alexandra, from the Greek, help of men

ALFREDA: (Teut.-Ang.-Sax.) wise counsel

ALLEGRA: (It.) cheerful; comforter

ALMETA: (Lat.) forward to the goal; brisk and industrious

ALMIRA: (Arab.) the exalted one, princess; (Hin.) a receptacle for clothing

ALODIA, ALODIE: (Lat.-Teut.) wealth; a prosperous woman

ALOYSIA: (Teut.) feminine form of Aloysius, famous war-maid

ALPHA: (Gr.) first

ALPHONSINE: (Teut.) nobly ready and eager for war

ALVA, ALVINA: (Lat.) the sedge; (Span.) white

ALVITA: (Lat.-Teut.) full of life, vivacious

ALYSIA: (Gr.) a chain, unbroken bond, possessive

ALYSSA: (Gr.) a flower name; probably derived from Alysson, a plant reputed to cure madness

ALZENA: (Arab.) woman

AMABEL, AMABELLA, AMABELLE: (Lat.) loved one, lovable creature

AMADEA: (Lat.) loving God, to love God

AMALABERTA: (Teut.) bright worker

AMALBURGA: (Teut.) a bright nature

AMANTA: (Lat.) loving

AMARIS: (Heb.) the promised one; (Lat.) child of the moon

AMBER: (Arab.) originally from Ambergris, now applied to yellowish fossil resin; the yellow one

AMBROSINE: (Gr.) feminine form of Ambrose—immortal

AMELINA, AMELITA: (Gr.) derivatives of Amelia, energetic

AMENA: (Celt.) honest

AMETHYST: (Lat.) sobering; (Gr.) the sober one. A quartz anciently supposed to prevent drunkenness

AMORET, AMORETTE: (Lat.) little darling, sweetheart; a love-knot. Related to Italian Amoretto and French amour

AMORITA: (Lat.) she who is beloved

AMINTA: (Gr.) protection

ANCELIN: (Lat.) servant, handmaid

ANDROMEDA: (Gr.) man-ruler. In mythology princess rescued by Perseus

ANEIRA: (Wel.) truly white or truly golden

ANGWEN, ANNWEN: (Wel.) very beautiful

ANIELA: angel; from Italian Angelo

ANNONA: (Lat.) fruitful one

ANNORA: (Gr.) light; (Heb.) grace, as with Ann

ANSELMA: (Teut.) divine protectress

ANTOINETTE: (Gr.) a girl in bloom

ANWYL: (Wel.) dear

APRIL: (Lat.) the fertile one; to open as nature in spring

AQUILA: (Lat.) eagle

AQUILINA: (Lat.) little eagle

ARA: (Lat.) an altar

ARABELLA: (Teut.) beautiful eagle

ARAMINTA: origin obscure; probably a conjunction of Ara (altar) and Moneta (coinage of money). A free translation would be sacred coinage

ARDATH: (Heb.) flowering field

ARDDUN: (Wel.) sublime

ARDELIA: (Lat.) zealous

ARDINE: (Gr.) she who satisfies. From the word meaning to water, to quench

ARDIS: (Lat.) ardent gratifier

ARDRA: (Lat.) she who is ardent, or desirous

ARETA: (Gr.) maiden of virtue

ARETHUSA: (Gr.) virtuous. In mythology a nymph who was saved from her pursuers by being changed into a fountain

ARIANWEN: (Wel.) silvery-white

ARIEL: (Heb.) lion of God; sometimes referred to as the spirit of air, as in "The Tempest" by Shakespeare

ARIELLA: (Heb.) hearth of God

ARMILDA: (Teut.) armed battle-maid

ARMILLA, ARMIL: (Lat.) bracelet, armlet

ARMILLETTE: (Lat.) the gentle embracer; derived from armilla, bracelet or armlet

ARMINE, ARMINEL: (Ang.-Sax.) universal

ARMOREL: (Gael.) dweller by the sea

ARNHILDA: (Teut.) eagle battle-maid

ARNOLDINE: (Teut.) the eagle's mate

ARTEMA: (Gr.) moon goddess

ARTEMISIA: (Gr.) perfect one

ARVA: (Teut.) lofty powers

ASPASIA: (Gr.) radiant as a star

ASTRA, ASTREA: (Gr.) shining star

ASTRELLA, ASTRELLITA: (Gr.) little star

ATALANTA: (Gr.) delicate huntress

ATALIE: (Scan.) innocent maiden

ATHALIA, ATHALIAH: (Heb.) God is mighty and exalted

ATHENA: (Gr.) a woman of wisdom

ATHENE: (Gr.) goddess of wisdom; goddess of Athens

AUBERTA: (Teut.) bright, fair girl; a variant of Alberta

AUREA: (Lat.) golden

AURELIA: (Lat.) the golden one

AVISSA: (Lat.) maiden of bird-like delicacy

AVONWY: (Wel.) dweller by the river

AWEL: (Wel.) breeze, zephyr

AYLWEN: (Wel.) fair of brow

AZARIA: (Heb.) blessed of God

AZARINE: (Teut.) noble woman

AZURA: (Arab.-Pers.) blue

B

BAPTISTA, BATISTA: (Gr.) baptized (in the Lord's name)

BASSANIA: (Gr.) of the deep-sea realm

BATHILDA: (Teut.) commanding maid of battle

BATHSHEBA: (Heb.) daughter of the oath

BEATA: (Lat.) blessed

BEKA: (Heb.) half-sister

BELDA: (Old Fr.) beautiful woman; (Teut.) good mother

BENA: (Heb.) wise; (N.A. Ind.) the pheasant

BENEDICTA, BENICE: (Lat.) she who is blessed

BERNADETTE: (Teut.) the courageous little one

BERNADINE: (Teut.) bold, masterful; feminine form of Bernard

BERNESSA: (Teut.) maid of the bear strain; valorous. (From bera, meaning bear)

BERNETTE: (Teut.) brave little maid

BETHESDA: (Heb.) house of mercy

BILLIE: (Teut.) feminine form of William

BLODEYN: (Wel.) flower

BLODWEN: (Wel.) flower-white

BLYTHE: (Ang.-Sax.) joyous; friendly

BONNIE, BONNY: (Ang.-Sax.) good; (Gael.) pretty. (Probably from the French bonne —pretty one)

BRANWEN, BRANGWIRIN: (Wel.) little raven

BRENNA: (Celt.) the dark-haired; (Slav.) maiden with raven hair

BRONYA: (Rus.) armour

BURNETTA: (Old Fr.) little brown one

CALLIOPE: (Gr.) beautiful voice; muse of heroic poetry

CALLISTA: (Gr.) of great beauty

CALLUELLA: (Gr.) extremely beautiful

CALLULA: (Gr.) beauty

CALOSA: (Gr.) beautiful to behold

CALTHA: (Lat.) a marigold

CALVINA: (Lat.) bright-haired

CANDA: (Cymric) brightness

CANDACE: (Lat.) glowing

CANNA: (Lat.) a reed or cane; flower name

CAPELLA: (Lat.) a star in the constellation of Auriga

CARIN: (Lat.) keel

CARISSA: (Lat.) dear little schemer

CARLA: (Teut.) virile; diminutive form of Caroline, Carolyn

CARLETTA: (Teut.) little virile one

CARME: (Gr.) in classic mythology, a nymph

CARMIA: (Lat.) rosy

CASILDA: (Span.) the solitary one

CASIMIRA: (Lat.) bearer of peace

CASSIA: (Gr.) the cassia tree

CASSIOPEIA: (Gr.) fragrance of flowers; mother of Andromeda

CASTA, CASTARA: (Lat.) chaste

CATALINA: (Span.) a small parrot

CATHABELL: (Gr.-Lat.) pure beauty

CATHLIN: (Celt.) beautiful eyes

CATRIONA: probably a Scottish variant of Catharine, from the Greek meaning pure

CATTIMA: (Lat.) slender reed

CEDRELA: (Lat.) the silver fir

CEIN: (Celt.) jewel

CELENA: (Gr.) dark

CELESTA, CELESTE, CELESTINE: (Lat.) heavenly

CELO: (Gr.) flaming

CENTELLA: (Lat.) flashing light

CERELIA: (Lat.) pertaining to Ceres, goddess of grain and harvests; fruitful woman

CERRITA: (Span.) closed; sealed lips

CERYLE: (Lat.) a sea bird

CHANDRA: (Sans.) a goddess brighter than the stars; destroyer of evil

CHANTESUTA: (N.A. Ind.) firm of heart

CHAREMON: (Gr.) the spirit rejoicing

CHARIS: (Gr.) in mythology one of the three Graces; giver of graciousness to life

CHARITY: (Lat.) charitable; giver of love

CHARMAINE: (Lat.) little song

CHASTINE: (Lat.) pure

CHAVVAH: (Heb.) giver of life

CHENOA: (N.A. Ind.) white dove

CHIARA: (It.) famous

CHILALI: (N.A. Ind.) snowbird

CHIMALIS: (N.A. Ind.) bluebird

CHIQUITA: (Span.) little

CHISPA: (Span.) a spark

CHITSA: (N.A. Ind.) fair one

CHLORINE: (Gr.) golden green

CHO: (Jap.) butterfly

CHOLENA: (N.A. Ind.) bird

CHRESTELLA: (Gr.) good; worthy

CHRISTEL: (Gr.) ice-like

CHRISTIANE: (Gr.) a Christian

CHRYSILLA: (Gr.) golden-haired

CHUN: (Chin.) spring

CLADONIA: (Gr.) a branch (of a tree or plant)

CLAIRINE: (Lat.) bright maid

CLARESTA: (Lat.) bright glory

CLARETTE: (Lat.) little bright one

CLARIMOND: (Lat.) world-famed

CLARINITA: (Lat.) famous little one

CLEANTHA: (Gr.) famous bloom

CLEARESTA: (Gr.) highest peak of glory

CLEINE: (Gr.) famous

CLEODORA: (Gr.) glorious gift

CLEONIMIA: (Gr.) glorious name

CLEOPATRA: (Gr.) from a famous father

CLEOPHILA: (Gr.) lover of glory

CLEOSA: (Gr.) famous

CLEVA: (Lat.) a hilltop or cliff

CLORINDA: (Pers.) renowned

CLYMENIA: (Gr.) famous

CLYTE: (Gr.) in mythology, a maiden whom the gods turned into a sunflower— hence, looking to the sun

COLINETTE: (Lat.) a small dove

COLUMBIA: (Lat.) a dove

COMFORT: (Old Eng.) consolation; compassion. A name favoured by the Puritans

CONCEPTION: (Lat.) fruitful; sometimes used in honour of the Immaculate Conception

CONCESSA: (Lat.) granting of a favour

CONCETTA: (It.) an ingenious idea

CONCHA: (Lat.) a sea-shell

CONCORDIA: (Lat.) harmony; agreeable

CONNAL: (Lat.) faithful

CONRADINE: (Teut.) wise counsel

CONSUELA, CONSUELO: (Lat.) one who consoles

CORAH: (Hin.) constant

CORAL: (Gr.) from the sea coral

CORDANA: (Teut.) harmonizing

CORETTA: (Gr.) little maiden

CORINNA: (Gr.) maiden

CORLA: (Old Eng.) the curlew

COROLLA: (Lat.) a small crown

CORRA: (Celt.) a mountain glen

COSETTE: (Teut.) a pet lamb

COTTINA: (Gr.) crown of wild flowers

COULAVA: (Celt.) soft-handed

COYETTA: (Teut.) caged

COYNE: (Old Fr.) reserved, modest

CRESENTIA: (Lat.) of the half-moon

CRESSA: (Teut.) water-cress

CYRENE: (Gr.) a river nymph

DABARATH, DABERATH: (Heb.) from a cool part

DACIA: (Lat.) from afar

DAFFODIL: (Gr.) flower name of the lily family, especially the Asphodel

DAGNA: (Teut.) radiant as the day

DAKAPAKI: (N.A. Ind.) a blossom

DALE: (Teut.) dweller in a vale between hills

DALLAS: (Teut.) playful; (Cymric) skilful

DALTA: (Gael.) a pet child

DAMALIS: (Gr.) mild conqueror

DAMASA: (Old Fr.) damsel

DANAE: (Gr.) in mythology favourite of Jupiter and mother of Perseus; golden shower

DANELLA: (Teut.) wise mistress

DANETTE: (Heb.) God judges me; (Teut.) little mistress

DANICA: (Slav.) morning star

DANILA: (Heb.) God judges

DARAKA: (Sans.) mild; timid

DARCIE: (Celt.) dark

DARDA: (Hung.) a dart; (Heb.) pearl of wisdom

DARE: (Gr.) defiance

DARIA: (Pers.) one who has knowledge

DAVITA: (Heb.) the beloved

DAWN: (Teut.) break of day

DEA: (Lat.) goddess

DEADORA: (Lat.-Gr.) gift of the goddess

DEIPHILA: (Gr.) divine love

DELAMAY: (It.) of the spring

DELAROSA: (It.) of the rose

DELFINA: (Teut.) elfish

DELICIA: (Lat.) delicately pleasant

DELIE: (Old Fr.) delicate; slender

DELILAH: (Heb.) alluring; temptress

DELINDA: (Teut.) gentle

DELIZEA: (It.) delight

DELORA: (Lat.) from the sea-coast

DELPHIA: (Gr.) pertaining to the Oracle of Delphi

DELPHINIA: (Gr.) loving sister

DELTA: (Gr.) the fourth; fourth letter of the Greek alphabet

DEMA: (Ang.-Sax.) an arbiter

DEMETER: (Gr.) fertile; goddess of the harvest

DENA: (N.A. Ind.) a valley

DENANEER: (Arab.) piece of gold

DESIDERIA: (Lat.) desirable

DESIRATA: (Lat.) desired

DESMA: (Gr.) child of a bond

DESMONDA: (Teut.) divinely protected

DEVI: (Hin.) a goddess

DEVINA: (Lat.-Teut.) divine

DEVNET: (Celt.) white wave

DEVONA: (Teut.) defensive; brave maid

DEVOTA: (Lat.) pious

DEXTRA: (Lat.) dexterous

DI: (Lat.) goddess; (Celt.) fire

DIADEMA: (Gr.) a diadem; badge of loyalty

DIAMANTA: (Lat.) of the diamond

DIANEME: (Gr.) of divine origin

DIANTHE: (Gr.) divine flower; flower of the pink species

DIAPHENIA: (Gr.) transmitting light

DICENTRA: (Gr.) flower name; known in old-fashioned gardens as bleeding heart

DIELLA: (Lat.) worshipper of God

DIERA: (Teut.) precious

DIGNA: (Lat.) worthy

DINORAH: origin obscure; title of opera by Meyerbeer

DIONE: (Gr.) goddess of moisture

DIONETTE: (Gr.) little Dione

DIVA: (Lat.) a goddess. In modern usage, a prima donna

DOCILA, DOCILLA: (Lat.) flexible; willing to learn

DODO: (Heb.) loving

DOLFINE: (Teut.) noble wild one

DOMINA: (Lat.) mistress; lady of the household

DOMINICA: (Lat.) a child born on Sunday

DONABELLA: (Lat.) beautiful lady

DONALDA: (Celt.) little mistress

DONATA: (Lat.) a gift

DONELLA: (Lat.) little damsel

DORDIA: (Gr.-Heb.) gift from the Almighty

DOREA: (Gr.) a bounty; a gift

DORENA: (Gr.) bountiful

DORENN: (Celt.) sullen

DORHISSA: (Heb.) gift of the oath

DORINA: (Heb.) perfection

DORITA: (Gr.) giver

DORYMENE: (Gr.) courageous

DOVA: (Teut.) dove, the emblem of peace and gentleness

DROMICIA: (Gr.) swift

DUSA: (Slav.) happy

DYANI: (N.A. Ind.) a deer

DYSIS: (Gr.) sunset

EASTER: (Ang.-Sax.) young as the springtime

EDBURGA: (Ang.-Sax.) noble protection

EDGARDA: (Teut.) rich battle-maid

EDGINA: (Teut.-Gr.) born to wealth

EDLA: (Teut.) a woman of noble family

EDMEE: (Ang.-Sax.) fortunate protector

EDMONDA: (Teut.) happy protector; (Ang.-Sax.) the hand of happiness

EDRA: (Teut.) rich wisdom; (Heb.) woman of power

EDRIA: (Teut.) wealthy

EGBERTA: (Teut.) formidably bright

EGLANTYNE: (Eng.) plant name

EGLATINE: (Teut.) the sweet briar

EILIEN: (Gr.) light

ELAMA: (Gr.) from the highland

ELATA: (Lat.) exultant

ELBERTA: (Teut.) nobly bright

ELDORA: (Teut.) gift of wisdom

ELDREDA, ELDRIDA: (Ang.-Sax.) wise friend

ELECTRA: (Gr.) yellow-haired

ELETA: (Span.) the astonished

ELGA: (Ang.-Sax.) little fighter

ELGIVA: (Teut.) gift of the elves

ELINEL: (Celt.) shapely

ELITA: (Teut.) the chosen

ELLADORA: (Teut.) gift of the elves

ELLORA: (Gr.) happy

ELODIE: (Gr.) fragile flower

ELOYS: (Teut.) famed holiness

ELPHIA: (Gr.) ivory

ELRA: (Teut.) elfin wisdom

ELRICA: (Teut.) regal

ELVARETTA: (Teut.-Gr.) virtue

ELVERDA: (Gr.) the virgin

ELVETTA: (Teut.) wise little home-ruler

ELVIA: (Teut.) of keen mind

ELVINA: (Teut.) wise and friendly

ELWY: (Wel.) benefit

ELWYN: (Wel.) white-browed

ELYSIA: (Lat.-Gr.) of paradise; divinely happy

EMANUELA: (Heb.) God is with thee

EMINA: (Teut.) prominent

EMOGENE: (Gr.) beloved child

EMRYS(S): (Celt.) immortal

ENDA: (Sans.) the last

ENFYS: (Wel.) rainbow

ENGRACIA: (Lat.) graceful

ENONE: (Gr.) wayside flower

ERASMA: (Gr.) desired

ERDA: (Teut.) worldly

ERIANTHE: (Gr.) sweetness of many flowers

ERINNA: (Celt.) peace

ERLINA: (Ang.-Sax.) little elf

ERLINDA: (Heb.) lively

ERMA: (Teut.) noble maid

ESTRELLA: (Span.) pertaining to star

ESWEN: (Wel.) strength

ETHELIND: (Teut.) wise judge of people

ETHELINDA: (Ang.-Sax.) gracefully noble

EUCLEA: (Gr.) glorious

EUCLIDA: (Gr.) the calculating one

EUDOCIA: (Gr.) proven of high standard; well-taught by a wise father

EUDORA: (Gr.) of fine gifts

EURWEN: (Wel.) golden-fair

EUSTACIA: (Gr.) fruitful

EVADNE: (Gr.) fortunate

EVANIA: (Gr.) obedient

EVANTHE: (Gr.) lovely flower; she who is well decorated

EVELYN: (Lat.) hazel nut; (Celt.) lively, pleasant; a variant of Eveleen

EVODIE: (Gr.) she who takes the right path

EZARA: (Heb.) little treasure

FABIA: (Lat.) Roman family name, signifying bean-grower

FABIOLA: (Lat.) woman of good works. Became popular in some religious families after publication in 1854 of book of same name, by Cardinal Wiseman

FABRIANNE: (Lat.) young woman of good works

FAE: (Old Fr.) she who trusts

FAINE: (Ang.-Sax.) joyful

FANSHOM: (Teut.) free

FARICA: (Teut.) peace-loving ruler

FAUSTA, FAUSTINE: (Lat.) fortunate

FAWNIA: (Ang.-Sax.) joyous one

FELDA: (Teut.) inspired; (Ang.-Sax.) of the open country

FELIPA: (Gr.) lover of horses

FENELLA: (Celt.) white-shouldered

FERNON: (Teut.) distant

FERONIA: (Lat.) a goddess presiding over forests

FIFINELLA: (Fr.-It.) another form of Fifi, the French pet form of Josephine

FINGAL: (Celt.) fair stranger

FINLEY: (Gael.) sunbeam

FINNA: (Celt.) white

FILIPA: (see Felipa)

FIONNA: (Celt.) ivory-skinned

FLETA: (Teut.) swift as an arrow; (Ang.-Sax.) fragrantly beautiful

FLEUR: (Fr.) flower

FLORANTHE: (Lat.-Gr.) flower-blossom

FLORETTA, FLORETTE: (Lat.) little flower

FLORIMEL: (Lat.-Gr.) honey-flower

FLUR: (Celt.) a flower

FONDA: (Lat.) deep, profound woman

FORTUNA: (Lat.) goddess of fortune; lucky

FOSSETTA: (Fr.) dimpled

FRANCESCA: (It.) form of Frances, free

FREA: (Scan.) lady

FREDELLA: (Teut.) peaceful elf

FREDICIA: (Teut.) peace-ruler

FREDLINA: (Teut.) wise and peaceful

FRESA: (Teut.) curly-haired

FREYA: (Scan.) a lady of love; Norse goddess of love and beauty

FRIDESWIDE: (Ang.-Sax.) peaceably strong

FRITZIE: (Teut.) peaceful ruler

FRODINE: (Teut.) wise friend

FROMA: (Teut.) holy

FULCA: (Lat.) accomplished, capable

GAERWEN: (Wel.) a place-name; literally white fort
GAIA: (Gr.) earth
GALE: (Ang.-Sax.) pleasant, happy; a pet form of Abigail
GAMBLE: (Scan.) old
GARDENIA: (Eng.) after the flower-name
GARLANDA: (Lat.) adorned with flowers
GARNET: (Lat.) like the precious gem; (Teut.) a jewel (also a male name)
GASPARINE: (Pers.) a horse-woman
GAVIOTA: (Span.) sea-gull
GAVRA: (Heb.) God is my rock
GAY: probably a diminutive of the French, Gayla; or direct from the adjective
GAYLA: (Fr.) the joyous one (from Gai); (Teut.) merry
GAYNA: probably a form of Guinevere

GELASIA: (Gr.) laughing girl
GEMINI: (Gr.) born in May; twin
GEMMA: (Lat.) a gem
GENESIA: (Lat.) newcomer
GENEVA: (Teut.) a distilled spirit
GENEVRA: probably another form of Guinevere
GERALDA: (Teut.) courageous
GERMAINE: (Teut.) akin, belonging
GIACINTA: (Gr.) dark flower
GIANINA: (Heb.) the Lord's grace
GILBERTA: (Teut.) bright pledge
GILMORY: (Celt.) Mary's servant
GINA: (Jap.) silvery
GINGER: (Lat.) pet form of Virginia—a maid, virgin
GISALA, GISELA: (Teut.) a pledge
GITHA: (Ang.-Sax.) war
GITTA: (Heb.) goodness
GITTLE: (Heb.) innocent flatterer
GLEDA: (Ice.) make glad
GLENDA: (Wel.) holy

GLENIS, GLENYS: (Wel.) good, pure

GLENNA: (Gael.) a valley maiden

GLINDA: origin unknown; probably a variant of Glenda

GLINYS: (Wel.) little valley

GLORIANA: (Lat.-Heb.) glorious grace

GLYNIS: see Glinys

GODEBERTA: (Teut.) divine brightness; (Lat.) a girl who serves God

GODELEVA: (Lat.) a girl of God's brightness

GODINE: (Teut.) God's friend

GOEWIN, GOEWYN: (Wel.) sprightly

GONERIL: (Lat.) honoured

GRACIA, GRATIA: (Lat.) favour, grace, the graceful one

GRACIOSA: (Span.) gracefully attractive

GRAINE: (Celt.) love

GRANIA: (Celt.) affectionate love

GRATIANA: the grateful Anne

GRAZINA: (It.) grace, favour, charm

GREDEL: (Teut.) the pearl

GREER: (Gr.) the watchwoman

GREGORIA: (Gr.) the watcher

GRETEL: a variant of Gredel

GRIMONIA: (Lat.) venerable woman

GRISELDA: (Teut.) indomitable maid (Some authorities give it as stone of heroism)

GRISELDIS: (Teut.) grey battlemaid

GRIZEL, GRISELL: variants of Griseldis

GROVENA: (Teut.) dweller of the grove

GRYTA: (Lit.) good

GUDILA: (Teut.) God helps

GUDRID: (Teut.) divine impulse

GUDULA: (Lat.) good daughter

GUIDA: (Celt.) sensible; (Teut.) a guide

GUINEVERE: (Wel.-Ang.-Sax.) the fair wife; (Celt.) white wave

GULLA: (Scan.) yellow

GUNDRED: (Teut.) wise and brave

GUNHILD, GUNHILDA: (Teut.) battlemaid in war

GUNI: (Teut.) divine freshness

GWENDYDD: (Wel.) star of morning

GWENEAL: (Celt.) white angel

GWENNOL: (Wel.) the swallow

GWENOG: (Wel.) smiling

GWLITHYN: (Wel.) dew-drop

GWYLFAI: (Wel.) festival of May

GWYNNE: (Celt.) white

GYDA: (Teut.) gift

GYPSY: wanderer; origin not definite, but probably Indian

GYTHA: (Ang.-Sax.) war

HADRIA: (Lat.) of the Adriatic

HAFWEN: (Wel.) beauty of summer

HAGGAI: (Heb.) one who is festive

HALCYON: (Lat.-Gr.) calm, peaceful. Thought to have come from halsion, a kingfisher which nested on a calm sea

HALDIS: (Teut.) spirit of the stone; firm

HALENA: (Slav.-Gr.) light

HALETTE: (Ang.-Sax.) tiny queen

HALIMEDA: (Gr.) sea-moss

HALONA: (N.A. Ind.) happy, fortunate times

HAMELINE: (Teut.) fond of home

HANA: (Jap.) flower

HANUSIA: (Heb.) grace of the Lord

HARELDA: (Scan.) sea duck

HARMONIA: (Gr.) unity

HARRIET: (Teut.) mistress of the home

HARU: (Jap.) spring

HASITA: (Sans.) laughing

HATTIE, HATTY: diminutive forms of Harriet

HEBE: (Gr.) personification of youth. In mythology goddess of youth; cupbearer to the gods

HEDDA: (Teut.) a haven in trouble; derived from Hedwig.

HEDONA: (Gr.) extreme delight

HEDVA: (Gr.) industrious worker

HEDWIG: (Teut.) haven in trouble

HEDY: (Teut.) a pet form of Hedwig

HELBONA: (Heb.) fruitful

HELIANTHE: (Gr.) bright flower; sunflower

HELISE: (Gr.) of the Elysian fields

HELMA: (Ang.-Sax.) a helm or rudder; (Teut.) helmet

HELONIA: (Gr.) a marsh lily

HELSA: (Heb.) given to God

HENDRIKA: (Teut.) ruler of the home

HERA: (Gr.) heroine; protector of women. In Greek mythology Hera (or Here) goddess of marriage

HERMA: (Teut.) beloved

HERMANDINE: (Teut.) a warrior's sweetheart

HERMIA: (Gr.) stately

HERO: (Gr.) in mythology beloved of Leander, for whom he swam the Hellespont; sometimes given as mistress of the house

HESPER: (Gr.) night star

HESTIA: (Gr.) in mythology goddess of the hearth

HEULWEN: (Wel.) sunshine

HIBERNIA: (Lat.) Ireland

HOLLY: (Ang.-Sax.) holy; English plant-name associated with Christmas

HONESTA: (Lat.) honourable

HONORA: (Lat.) a symbol of honour

HOSEA: (Heb.) salvation

HUBERTA: (Teut.) bright in spirit; feminine form of Hubert

HUGA: (Teut.) intellectual

HUGUETTE: (Teut.) feminine form of Hugh—thoughtful, intellectual

I

IANTHINE: (Gr.) like the violet

ICASIA: (Teut.) god-like; (Gr.) happy

IDALAH: (Heb.) one who proceeds softly or snares

IDALINE: (Gr.) the far-seeing

IDELIA: (Teut.) noble

IDELLE: (Gr.-Teut.) clever, happy one

IDINA: (Scan.) work

IDMONIA: (Gr.) skilful

IDOLA: (Lat.) idolized

IDONEA: (Lat.) proper; (Scan.) Norse spring goddess

IDONETTE: (Lat.) proper little lady who never works

IGNATIA: (Lat.) the fiery, or ardent one

IGNES: (Lat.) pure

ILA: (Ang.-Sax.) insulate; island-dweller

ILDE: (Teut.) battlemaid

ILONE: (Hung.) radiant beauty; (Gr.) light

IMOGENA, IMOGENE: (Lat.) visionary; an image; (Gr.) beloved child

IMPERIA: (Lat.) imperious

INEZ: (Gr.) pure

INGA: (Teut.) dweller in the meadow

INGEBORG: (Teut.) tower of protection

INNOCENTIA: (Lat.) unknowing of evil

IOLE: (Gr.) cloud at dawn

IONA: (Gr.) violet jewel; Greek flower-name

IORWEN: (Wel.) lord; beautiful

IPHIGENIA: (Gr.) of a royal and courageous race

IRETTE: (Teut.) little wrathful one

IRIAN: (Gr.) rare

IRMA: (Teut.) maid of high degree

IRMADEL: (Teut.) noble maiden

IRMALEE: (Teut.) Irma of the meadow

IRMIN: (Lat.) regal; a variant of ermine, the royal fur

ISADORA: (Gr.) a gift

ISAURA: (Gr.) soft air

ISCAR: (Heb.) she who watches

ISLA: (Old Fr.) island; (Lat.) insular

ISLAMEY: (Arab.) obedient to the will of Allah

ISLEAN: (Celt.) of sweet voice

ISMENA: (Gr.) learned one

ISOLA: (Lat.) alone; set apart

ITA: (Celt.) thirsty one

IVA: (Rus.) willow

IVENA: (Heb.) grace of the Lord

JACQUETTE: (Heb.) the little supplanter

JANNAH: (Heb.) the Lord graciously gave

JARITA: (Hin.) motherly devotion

JARVIA: (Old Eng.) feminine form of Jarvis—a driver

JASMINE: (Pers.) from Yasmin; flower name

JAVOTTE: (Celt.) white stream or wave

JEANNETTE: a variant of Jean, which is a Scottish form of Jane (Heb.) meaning grace of God

JELENA: (Gr.) light

JERUSHA: (Heb.) the exiled; some references give this as possession

JESKA: (Heb.) she who looks out

JESSLYN, JESSELINE: (Heb.) wealthy woman

JEVERA: (Heb.) life

JEWEL: (Old Fr.) joy

JOCUNDA: (Lat.) mirthful

JODETTE: (Lat.) sportive one

JODIS: (Teut.) horse sprite

JOFRID: (Teut.) lover of horses

JONEA: (Heb.) the Lord's grace

JORDANA: (Heb.) descendant

JORNA: (Span.) a journeyer

JOSCELIND: (Lat.) gentle playmate

JOVITA: (Lat.) merry; derived from Jove (Jupiter)

JOYAN: (Old Fr.) rejoicing

JUNIATA: (Lat.) ever youthful

JUNILLA: (Lat.) little maid who is ever youthful

JUNO: heavenly; in Roman mythology the wife of Jupiter

JUSTICIA: (Lat.) the just

JUSTINE: (Lat.) the righteous one

JUVENTIA: (Lat.) goddess of youth

KACHINA: (N.A. Ind.) sacred dance

KALAMA: (N.A. Ind.) the wild goose

KALMA: (Teut.) calm

KALONICA: (Gr.) the victory of beauty

KALYA: (Sans.) healthy

KALYANA: (Sans.) one who is virtuous

KALYCA: (Gr.) rosebud

KAMA: (Sans.) desired

KAMAMA: (N.A. Ind.) butterfly

KARINA: (Gr.) a variation of Katherine, pure

KARMA: (Sans.) destiny

KASAMIRA: (Slav.) peace-maker

KASIA: (Gr.) pure

KAULIKA: (Sans.) nobly born

KAYA: (N.A. Ind.) little elder sister

KENDRA: (Ang.-Sax.) a wo-man of knowledge; (Teut.) understanding

KESHENA: (N.A. Ind.) swift in flight

KETURAH: (Heb.) fragrance

KEVALA: (Sans.) one's own

KEYNE: (Celt.) jewel

KEZIAH: (Heb.) the cassia tree

KIARA: (It.) illustrious

KIM: origin unknown; prob-ably from Welsh war-chief

KINA: (Gr.) Christian mes-senger

KINETA: (Gr.) active

KIRBY: (Ang.-Sax.) one from the church-town

KIRTLEY: (Teut.) a tunic

KLEANTHA: (Gr.) celebrated flower

KLYMENA: (Gr.) celebrated

KOA: (Heb.) princess

KOLFINNA: (Celt.) cool, white lady

KOLINA: (Gr.) pure

KOLOTOSA: (N.A. Ind.) star

KOMALA: (Sans.) charming

KOREN: (Gr.) a maiden

KOTSASI: (N.A. Ind.) white flower

KYLA: (Gael.) comely
KYNA: (Gr.) lady

LABANA: (Heb.) ivory goddess

LABITTA: (Lat.) the girl with the luscious lips; from labium, the lip

LADORNA: (Lat.) embellished

LAINA: (Teut.) denial

LALAGE: (Gr.) a prattler, talkative one

LALITA: (Sans.) the pleasing, cherished one

LANA: (Lat.) the soft, woolly one; short form of Alana (Celt.)—my child

LARA: (Lat.) famous

LARENTIA: (Lat.) fostermother

LARINA: (Lat.) sea-gull; (Gr.) the plump one

LARISSA: (Lat.) the bright and shining one; in ancient Greece the chief town of Thessaly

LATONIA, LATONIE: (Lat.-Gr.) mother of Apollo; sometimes given as mother of the sun

LAUDA: (Lat.) praise

LAUDETTE: (Lat.) little praiseworthy one

LAVERNE: (Fr.) like the spring

LEAL: (Celt.) faithful

LEANNA, LEANNE: combination of Lee and Anna

LEATRICE: (Lat.) young and joyful

LEDA: (Heb.) beautiful temptress; in Greek mythology mother of Helen and Clytemnestra

LEFA: (Teut.) the heart of a plant or tree

LEILANI: (Haw.) heavenly flower

LEMMUELA, LEMUELA: (Heb.) devoted to God

LENI: a German diminutive of Magdalene

LENICE: (Gr.) feminine form of Leonard—brave as a lion

LENKA: (Slav.) light

LEODA: (Teut.) woman of the people

LEOLIE: (N.A. Ind.) prairie flower

LEONA: (Lat.-Fr.) feminine form of Leo—strong and brave as a lion

LEONTI(Y)NE: (Lat.) like a lioness

LEOPOLDINE: (Teut.) of bold people

LESBIA: (Gr.) a woman of the island of Lesbos

LETA: (Lat.) joyful

LEWANNA: (Heb.) the moon

LEWINA: (Heb.) little battle-prize

LIANA: (Lat.) a plant-name

LIBNA: (Heb.) fair

LILYBELLE: a combination of Lily and Belle; beautiful lily

LINDALOU: combination of Linda and Louise — war heroine

LINNEA: (Scan.) linden tree

LINTRUDE: (Teut.) of serpent strength

LIRA: (Gr.) lyre

LISLE: (Fr.) the island

LITA: diminutive of any name ending in lita

LIVIA: diminutive of Olivia, the olive tree, symbol of peace

LLAWELA: (Wel.) feminine form of Llewellyn, leader, lightning

LLINOS: (Wel.) the linnet

LOIETU: (N.A. Ind.) a flower; farewell to spring

LORI: (Flem.) the lazy one

LORIS: (Lat.) slow

LOTUS: (Egyp.) flower of forgetting

LUBA: (Ang.-Sax.-Slav.) my beloved

LUBRA: (Slav.) lover

LUCIDA: (Lat.) shining

LUCIOLA: (Lat.) a firefly

LUCIPPE: (Gr.) white horse

LUDMILLA: (Slav.) loved by the people

LUDWINIA: (Teut.) the people's friend

LULETTE: (Teut.) little comforter

LULITA: (Sans.) agitated

LUMAI: (N.A. Ind.) the humming of birds' wings

LUNA: (Lat.) shining; goddess of the half-moon

LUNETTA: (Lat.) little moon

LUPE: (Lat.) the wolfess; (Teut.) prophecy of good fortune

LYNN: (Gr.) a refreshing water pool

LYNNA: (Teut.) a cascade

LYRIS: (Gr.) song of the lyre

LYSANDRA: (Gr.) liberator

MABYN: (Wel.) youthful

MADHURA: (Sans.) charming

MADORA: (Gr.) my gift

MADRA: (Lat.) mother

MAE: (Ang.-Sax.) kinswoman

MAGASKI: (N.A. Ind.) white swan

MAGDA: form of Magdalene and Magdaline—see Magdala

MAGDALA: (Gr.) a tower; (Heb.) woman of Magdala

MAGNOLIA: an allusion to the tree and flower of that name,

so called in honour of Pierre Magnol, French botanist

MAHLAH: (Heb.) melodious song

MAHOLA: (Heb.) dancer

MAHSA: (Arab.) a little moon

MAIDA: (Teut.) maiden; place-name in Italy

MALCA: (Teut.) industrious

MALINDA: (Old Eng.) gentle

MALITA: (N.A. Ind.) salmon

MALTA: (Pho.) refuge

MALVA: (Gr.) the soft one; (Lat.) plant-name

MANNUELA: (Span.-Heb.) God is with us

MARABEL: (Fr.) beauteous Mary

MARELLA: (Heb.-Teut.) Mary of bright intellect

MARG, MARGOT: short form of Margaret—a pearl

MARIBELLE: see Marabel

MARIETTA: Italian diminutive of Mary—wished-for child

MARIGOLD(E): (Teut.) Mary's gold; (Ang.-Sax.) resplendent Mary

MARINA: (Lat.) maiden of the sea

MARMORA: (Gr.) radiant

MAROLA: (Lat.) she who lives by the sea

MARSHA: a variant of Marcia —brave

MARVA: (Lat.) wonderful

MATRONNA: (Lat.) motherly

MATTA: (Heb.) gift of the Lord

MAURILLA: (Teut.) wise, dark-eyed girl

MAURITA: (Lat.) little dark girl

MAXENTIA: (Lat.) of great talent

MAXIMA: (Lat.) greatest

MAYNA: (Teut.) home woman

MEDARDA: (Heb.) pearl of wisdom; (Lat.) scholar

MEDEA: (Gr.) the enchantress; she who rules

MEDIA: (Lat.) the centre

MEDITA: (Lat.) reflective

MEDORA: (Gr.) guardian; (Ang.-Sax.) patient wife

MEHETABEL, MEHITABEL: (Heb.) God benefits

MEINGOLDA: (Teut.) my golden flower

MEINWEN: (Wel.) slender

MELADA: (Gr.) honey

MELANTHA: (Gr.) dark or melancholy flower

MELEDA: (Teut.) chatterer

MELIA: (Gr.) the ash-tree

MELIANTHA: (Gr.) sweet flower

MELIKA: (Gr.) lyrical

MELINA: (Gr.) gentle

MELITA: (Lat.) sweet as honey; (Gr.) little honey flower

MELONIA: (Gr.) dark

MELOSA: (Gr.) melody

MERARI: (Gr.) she of sadness

MERAS: (Heb.) worthy

MERCEDES: (Lat.) a pleasing reward; (Span.) merciful

MERIDA: (Lat.) noonday

MERIEL: (Gr.) a variant of Muriel, fragrant, perfumed

MERRIE: (Ang.-Sax.) mirthful

MERRILA: (Gr.) fragrance

MERULA: (Lat.) blackbird

MERYL: (Gr.) the fragrant myrrh

META: (Lat.) a goal; turning point in a race

MIA: (Ital.-Span.) mine

MICHAELA: (Heb.) she who is like a goddess; divine

MIGNON: (Lat.) delicate; (Old Fr.) delicately formed

MIHEWI: (N.A. Ind.) sun-woman

MINERVA: (Lat.) the wise one

MIONE: (Gr.) small

MIRABEL, MIRABELLA, MIRABELLE: (Lat.) of great beauty

MIRU: (Slav.) harmony, peace

MITZI: pet form of Mary and Maria

MODANA: (Sans.) gladdening

MODESTA: (Lat.) modest

MODWEN, MODWENNA: (Wel.) maiden; queen

MORA: (Gael.) sun

MORIA: (Gr.) chosen by the Lord or fate

MOYNA: (Celt.) the gentle and soft

MOZA: (Heb.) fountain

MUSA: (Lat.) a song

MUSETTA: (Lat.) a little song

MUSIDORA: (Gr.) gift of the muses

MYFANWY: (Wel.) my rare one

NAAMA: (N.A. Ind.) pleasantness

NAARAH: (Heb.) girl of our hearts

NAHAMA, NAHAMAN: (Heb.) God's comfort

NAHTANHA: (N.A. Ind.) corn flower

NANINE: (Gr.) dainty little one

NARDA: (Gr.) the fragrant one; (Lat.) plant-name (spikenard from spica nardi)

NATA: (Sans.) dancer

NATHANIA: (Heb.) feminine form of Nathaniel

NEALA: (Gael.) feminine form of Neal, champion

NEDA: (Slav.) sabbath-born

NEOMA: (Gr.) the new moon

NETTA: (Gr.) the duckling; (Teut.) a net

NEVA: (Lat.) snow

NEVADA: (Lat.) snowy

NEYSA: (Gr.) chaste, pure

NICOLA, NICOLE: (Gr.) victor of the people; feminine form of Nicholas

NIDIA, NYDIA: (Lat.) the homemaker

NIGELLA: (Lat.) plant-name; black

NIPHA: (Gr.) a snowflake

NOLA, NOLANA: (It.) a little bell

NOLETA: (Lat.) the unwilling maiden

NONA: (Lat.) ninth; the ninth child

NORINE: (Lat.) honourable

NORNA: (Lat.-Scan.) a Norse fate (goddess)

NOVA, NOVIA: (Lat.) new

NUNCIATA: (Lat.) a form of Annunciata; messenger of a delightful promise

NYASSA: (Ang.-Sax.) sister; (Gr.) pierced

NYMPHODORA: (Gr.) gift of the nymphs; bride gift

OBALA: (Heb.) from the hills

OBELIA: (Gr.) a tall, pointed pillar

ODA: (Teut.) rich; (Lat.) a song

ODELET, ODELETTE: (Gr.-Lat.) a little song

ODELIA: (Dan.) the heiress; (Teut.) prosperous

OILIEN: (Rus.) deer

OLA: (Gr.) the virgin; (Heb.) eternal; (Scan.) daughter or descendant

OLATHE: (N.A. Ind.) beautiful

OLATTA: (N.A. Ind.) a lagoon

OLETHEA: (Gr.) gift of the gods; (Lat.) of truth

OLWEN: (Wel.) white footprint

ONA: (Lat.) a form of Una—meaning the one

ONDINE: (Lat.) see Undine

ONYX: (Gr.) jewel-name

OONAH: (Celt.) Irish form of

Una (Lat.) the one; expressive of perfection

OPAL: (Sans.) jewel, most beautiful of gemstones

OPHELIA: (Gr.) one who helps

ORA: (Gr.) that of beauty; (Lat.) to pray, to orate

ORDRICK: (Teut.) of kingly origin

ORELLA: (Lat.) she who listens

ORIANA: (Celt.) girl of the golden (or white) skin; (Lat.) risen

ORLANTHA: (Teut.) of wide fame

ORLENA, ORLINE: (Fr.) the golden maiden; (Lat.) of golden radiance

ORVA: (Teut.) golden; (Ang.-Sax.) a brave friend

ORVALA: (Lat.) of golden worth

OSELLA: (It.) a bird

OSYTH: (Ang.-Sax.) war-god

OTHA: (Teut.) prosperous

OTTA: (Ang.-Sax.) a mountain

OVINA: (Lat.) lamb-like

OWENA: (Wel.-Gr.) a feminine form of Owen, well-born

OWISSA: (N.A. Ind.) a bluebird; harbinger of spring

OZELLA: (Heb.) a shadow

PACIFICA: (Lat.) peaceable

PALLAS: (Gr.) the wise maiden

PALLUA: (Heb.) distinguished

PALMEDA: (Gr.) inventive

PALOMA: (Span.) a dove

PARTHENIA: (Gr.) a virgin

PAVITA: (Sans.) purified

PEACE: (Lat.-Old Fr.) happy freedom; a peaceful child

PELAGIA, PELAGIE: (Gr.) dweller by the sea

PENTHEA: (Gr.) fifth, the fifth child

PEONY: (Gr.) flower-name; probably named after Palon, physician to the gods

PEPITA: (Heb.) addition; (Span.) she who adds

PERIZADA: (Pers.) fairy-born

PERLITA: (It.) pearl

PERNELLE: (Gr.) stone or rock

PERPETUA: (Lat.) perpetual

PETULA: (Lat.) seeker

PHALOSA: (Gr.) shining

PHENICE: (Heb.) of the stately palm tree

PHILANA: (Heb.) loving grace

PHILANTHA: (Gr.) lover of flowers

PHILLIDA, PHILLINE: (Gr.) a loving woman

PHILOTHRA: (Gr.) pious

PHILYRIA: (Gr.) grace of the willow

PHOTINA, PHOTINE: (Gr.) light

PHRYNE: (Gr.) pale

PIA: (Lat.) pious

PIERETTE: a French diminutive of Pierre (Peter)—rock

PINON: (Gr.) pearl

PIPPA: an Italian diminutive of Philippa—lover of horses

PLACIDA: (Lat.) calm

POMONA: (Lat.) the delicious fruit; goddess of fruit

PORTIA: (Lat.) meaning obscure; some references give it as harbour-safety; others porcine

PRECIOSA: (Lat.) precious

PRIMA: (Lat.) the first; often given to the first child of the family

PRIMALIA: (Lat.) spring-like

PRIMAVERA: (Lat.) fragrant promise of youth; born in springtime

PRIYA: (Sans.) beloved

PROBA: (Lat.) honest

PULCHERIA: (Lat.) of great beauty

PYRENE: (Gr.) red-haired

PYTHIA: (Gr.) the high priestess; Apollo's priestess at Delphi

QUARTAS: (Lat.) the fourth (born)

QUERIDA: (Span.) the loved one

QUESTA: (Lat.) the plaintive song (note) of the nightingale

QUINTA, QUINTELLA, QUINTINA: (Lat.) the fifth

QUITERIA: (Lat.) vital

RADINKA: (Teut.) playful

RAHMA: (Arab.) divine mercy

RANA: (Hin.) royal

RAYMA: (Teut.) rambler

REBA: a short form of Rebecca

REDENTA: (Lat.) redeemed

REI: (Jap.) ceremonious

RENEE: (Fr.) born again

RENNAH: (Heb.) a ringing cry

RESEDA: (Lat.) dainty and graceful;

REVA: (Lat.) she who has been restored; (Old Fr.) a dreamer

REXANA: (Lat.-Heb.) regal grace

RHEA: (Gr.) she flows with honey and delight

RICARDA: (Lat.-Teut.) powerful; a woman fit for a king

ROANNA: (Heb.-Teut.) gracious

ROBIA: (Teut.) famous

ROBINA: (Teut.) a variant of Roberta, bright flame

ROCHANA: (Pers.) dawn of day

RODERICA: (Teut.) feminine form of Roderic(k)—rich in fame

ROLANDA: (Teut.) feminine form of Roland—fame of the land

ROMILDA: (Teut.) little brave battle-maid

ROSABEL, ROSABELLE: (Lat.) the beautiful rose

ROSARANA: (Celt.) the rosebush

ROSELLE: (Lat.) little rose

ROSEMARIE: (Lat.-Heb.) a variant of Rosemary, which has two meanings—dew of the sea, and Mary's rose

ROSGRANA: (Celt.) sunbeam

ROZENE: (N.A. Ind.) rose

RUCITA: (Sans.) glittering

RUELLA: (Teut.) lucky elfin one

RUFINA: (Lat.) reddish; red-haired

SABBA: (Heb.) rest

SABELLA: (Lat.) the wise

SACHARISSA: (Gr.) sweet

SAI: (Jap.) intelligence

SAMALA: (Sans.) tranquillizing

SAMARA: (Lat.) seed of the elm; (Heb.) the gentle guardian

SANCHIA: (Span.) holy

SAPPHIRA: (Heb.) the pretty one

SECUNDA: (Lat.) the second (child)

SEDA: (Arm.) echo through the woods

SELA: (Gr.) the shining one

SEMELE: (Lat.) the one and only; (Gr.) mythical daughter of Cadmus and Hermione whose graceful beauty aroused Juno's jealous rage

SEPTIMA: (Lat.) seventh (child)

SERICA: (Lat.) silken

SHADA: (N.A. Ind.) the pelican

SHEBA: (Heb.) bound by the vows of faithfulness

SHEDEA: (N.A. Ind.) wild sage

SHERYL: (Teut.) a variant of Shirley—meadow; sweet

SHIRLEEN: (Pers.) sweet

SHOHAN: (Heb.) pearl

SIDA: (Gr.) a water-lily

SIDRA: (Lat.) star-like

SOLAH: (Lat.) alone

SOLITA: (Lat.) little lonely one

SONIA: (Slav.) wise one; a Russian form of Sophia—wisdom

STACEY: (Gr.) a variant of Anastasia—resurrection

STELLA: (Lat.) star-like

STEPHANIE: (Gr.) a crown

SULA: (Ice.) the sun

SULWYN: (Wel.) fair as the sun

SWETLANA: (Teut.) a star

SYBIL: (Gr.) a wise woman

SYLVA: (Lat.) woodland

SYLVANA: (Lat.) of the woodland

T

TACITA: (Lat.) the silent one
TALITHA: (Arab.) graceful as the gazelle; (Arm.) fair damsel
TALLULAH: (N.A. Ind.) restless as running water
TANIA: a pet form of Tatiana
TATIANA: (Lat.) silver-haired
TEGAN: (Wel.) beautiful
TERRENA: (Lat.) of earthly pleasures
TERTIA: (Lat.) third (child)
THEOLA: (Gr.) deified; sent from God
THERA: (Gr.) the untamed; the phallically unconquered
THETIS: (Gr.) a sea nymph; in mythology the mother of Achilles
THOMASA, THOMASINA: (Arm.) a twin
TILDA, TILLIE, TILLY: (Teut.) variants of Mathillda, Matilda—mighty battlemaid

TITA: (Lat.) safe
TORA: (Scan.) dedicated to Thor, god of thunder
TRINA: (Gr.) woman of purity
TRINETTE: (Gr.) little girl of purity
TRISTA: (Lat.) the sorrowful one

U

UMA: (Sans.) light
UNDINE: (Lat.) of the waves; a water-sprite that can obtain a human soul by bearing a child to a human husband
URBANA: (Lat.) a polite, town-bred woman
UTINA: (N.A. Ind.) (woman of) my country
UDELE: (Teut.-Ang.-Sax.) the clever, rich one
ULA: (Celt.) jewel of the sea
ULMA: (Lat.) the elm tree
ULTIMA: (Lat.) the last

V

VALDA: (Teut.) inspiring in battle

VALENTINA: (Lat.) the strong and valorous one

VALMAI: (Wel.) May-flower

VALONIA: (Lat.) a maiden of the valley; (Gr.) seed of the oak

VANDA: (Teut.) kindred

VANIA: (Heb.) the grace of God; Russian equivalent of Jane

VASHTI: (Pers.) the best, the most beautiful

VEDA: (Sans.) the learned and wise one

VERDA: (Lat.) fresh and virginal

VERINA: origin obscure; probably a variant of Vera (Lat.) truth; (Rus.) faith

VINA: (Lat.) wine of life

VITA: (Lat.) the vital; full of life

VIVIA: (Lat.) lively

VOLETA, VOLETTA: (Old Fr.) veil; the veiled woman

W

WAHKUNA: (N.A. Ind.) beautiful

WENDELIN: (Ang.-Sax.) the wanderer

WENDY: origin obscure; probably from Gwendolen (Celt.), meaning white-bow

WENONA, WENONAH: (N.A. Ind.) the first-born daughter

WESLA: (Old Eng.) the girl from the west meadow

WETA: (Old Frie.) knowledge

WILDA: (Ang.-Sax.) the wild one

WILHELMINA: (Nor.) the helmet

WILLA: (Teut.) resolute

WINEMA: (N.A. Ind.) chieftainess

WINOLA: (Teut.) friendly princess

WINSOME: (Eng.) pleasantly attractive

WYANET: (N.A. Ind.) of great beauty
WYNNE: (Wel.) fair, blessed; (Teut.) the fulfilled wish

XANTHE: (Gr.) yellow; the yellow-haired
XYLIA: (Gr.) of a wood
XYLONA: (Gr.) a wood or forest dweller

YEDDA: (Teut.) singer
YETTA: (Heb.) mistress of the house

YOSHE: (Jap.) a beauty
YSIDORA: (Gr.) fair gift

ZADAH: (Arab.) prosperous
ZAMIRA: (Heb.) song
ZANA: (Pers.) woman
ZANETA: (Heb.) the grace of God
ZAREBA: (Sud.) an enclosure
ZELDA: a form of Griselda
ZELLA: (Heb.) a shadow
ZELOSA: (Gr.) jealous
ZENA: (Pers.) a woman
ZETA: (Gr.) a dwelling-place
ZITA: (Heb.) respected mistress
ZIVANA: (Slav.) animate

BOYS

AAHMES: (Egyp.) child of the moon

ABBOT: (Heb.) father of many; the male head of an abbey

ABDIEL: (Heb.) God's servant

ABIAH, ABIJAH: (Heb.) my father is the Lord

ABIEL: (Heb.) father of strength

ABIEZA: (Heb.) my father's help

ABITAL: (Heb.) father of the dew

ABRIC: (Teut.) beyond authority

ABROS: (Gr.) elegant

ACHATES: (Gr.) faithful companion

ACIMA: (Heb.) the Lord will judge

ACKERLEY: (Old Eng.) from the oak tree meadow

ADAIR: (Celt.) the oak tree ford

ADAL: (Teut.) noble

ADDIS: (Heb.-Eng.) an old contrived form of Adam

ADDISON: (Heb.) Adam's descendant

ADDO: (Teut.) noble cheer

ADELAR: (Teut.) noble eagle

ADELFRID: (Teut.) noble; peaceful

ADELGAR: (Teut.) bright or noble spear

ADELPHO: (Gr.) beloved brother

ADELWIN: (Teut.) noble friend

ADIEL: (Heb.) an ornament of God

ADIN: (Heb.) voluptuous

ADLAI: (Heb.) my ornament

ADLAR: (Teut.) an eagle

ADMETUS: (Teut.) untamed

ADNA: (Heb) pleasure

ADOETTE: (N.A. Ind.) big tree

ADONIS: (Gr.) adorned, of manly beauty; in mythology a hunter loved by Venus

ADRAH: (Heb.) ruler, prince

ADRASTUS: (Lat.-Gr.) inescapable

ADRIEL: (Heb.) one of God's flock

AELHAEARN: (Wel.) iron brow

AGAR: (Heb.) stranger

AGATHON: (Gr.) famed for kindness and goodness

AGILO: (Lat.) gleaming

AGNAR: (Teut.) undefiled

AHANU: (N.A. Ind.) one who laughs

AHEARN, AHERN: (Celt.) lord of the horses; (Wel.) iron

AHRENS: (Teut.) power of the eagle

AIDAN: (Gael.) fire

AIRELL: (Celt.) a free man

AJAX: (Gr.) earthy

AKIRA: (Jap.) intelligence

AKULE: (N.A. Ind.) he looks up

ALAND: (Celt.) bright as the sun

ALANUS: (Lat.) cheerful; (Celt.) in harmony

ALARD: (Teut.) nobly stern

ALAUDO: (Lat.) a lark

ALBAN: (Lat.) dawn of day, white

ALBER: (Teut.) agile of mind

ALBERIC: (Teut.) a ruler with bright, agile mind; elf-king

ALBERN: (Teut.) bear-like, brave

ALBIN: (Lat.) fair

ALBOR: (Lat.) dawn

ALBURN: (Lat.) pale

ALCANDER: (Gr.) manly

ALDEN: (Ang.-Sax.) old friend

ALDER: (Teut.) a tree of the genus Alnus

ALDO: (Teut.) steady; (Heb.) a servant

ALDRED: (Teut.) mature counsel

ALDRIDGE: (Teut.) dweller on the high ridge

ALDWIN: (Ang.-Sax.) old friend

ALEM: (Arab.) the one who has knowledge

ALI: (Arab.) servant

ALMER: (Arab.) a prince

ALMO: (Gr.) a river god

ALOIS: (Teut.) a form of Aloysius; famous warrior;

16th century Spanish saint

ALPHA: (Gr.) the first letter of the Greek alphabet; first-born

ALPHARD: (Arab.) solitary

ALPHEUS: (Gr.) god of the river

ALPIN: (Lat.) high, lofty

ALROY: (Lat.) royal; (Span.) king

ALSTON: (Ang.-Sax.) noble stone

ALVA: (Lat.-Span.) white

ALVAR: (Ang.-Sax.) elf enemy or elf army

ALVER: (Lat.) complete truth

ALVERNON: (Teut.-Lat.) of the springtime

ALVIS: (Scan.) wise suitor

ALWARD: (Teut.) protector of all

ALWORTH: (Teut.) respected by all

AMADEUS: (Lat.) the loving deity

AMADIS: (Lat.-Fr.) God love

AMALA: (Sans.) stainless

AMANDUS: (Lat.) worthy of love

AMIN: (Sans.) fruitful

AMINTAS: (Gr.) helpful

AMPARO: (Span.) defence; protection

ANARAWD: (Wel.) eloquent

ANATOLE: (Gr.) sunrise

ANCEL: (Teut.) godlike

ANDERS: (Scan.) courageous

ANDRIAS: (Gr.) courageous

ANDROS: (Gr.) manly

ANEURIN: (Wel.) of true gold

ANGWYN: (Wel.) very handsome

ANOKI: (N.A. Ind.) actor

ANSON: (Teut.) of divine origin; (Ang.-Sax.) the son of Ann

ARCO: (Lat.) an arch or arc

ARDEN, ARDIN: (Lat.) eager, fervent

ARDILLO: (Span.) a squirrel

ARDITH: (Old Fr.) flashing, fiery

ARI: (Teut.) eagle

ARIEL: (Heb.) lion of God

ARISTO: (Gr.) the best

ARISTOL: (Gr.) excellence

ARLES: (Scan.) a pledge

ARLETH: (Gr.) forgetful

ARLIN: (Teut.) sea-bound

ARLO: (Span.) the barbary;

(Old Eng.) the protected town

ARLYN: (Teut.) swift, like the cascade

ARMAND: (Teut.) a form of Herman; war or commanding man

ARMANDO: (Lat.) armed

ARMYN: (Teut.) a form of Armand

ARNO: (Lat.-Teut.) eagle

ARNVID: (Teut.) eagle of the forest

ARON: (Gr.) exalted

ARUNDEL: (Teut.) of the dell of eagles

ATHELSTONE, ANTHELSTAN: (Teut.) noble jewel or stone

ATHERTON: (Teut.) dweller in the woodland

ATHMORE: (Teut.) dweller in the heathland

AUBERT: (Teut.) fair ruler

AUDRIS: (Teut.) daring

AUDWIN: (Teut.) wealthy friend

AURIGA: (Lat.) charioteer

AURYN: (Wel.) gold

AVILA: (Span.) audacious

AYLA: (Gr.) of the woodland

AYLER: (Wel.) nobly renowned

AYLETT: (Lat.) a sea swallow

AYLSWORTH: (Teut.) of great wealth

AYMON: (Teut.) ruler of the home

AZAL: (Heb.) the mountain's foundation

AZAR, AZARIAH. AZARIAS: (Heb.) whom the Lord helps

AZEL: (Heb.) noble

BAILEY: (Teut.) the man in possession; (Fr.) an enclosure

BAINBRIDGE: (Gael.) of the sea

BAIRD: (Celt.) a variant of bard (singer)

BALDEMAR: (Teut.) of princely fame

BALDRIC: (Teut.) a warrior's belt or sash, denoting a brave soldier or prince; bold rule

BALIN: (Sans.) a soldier of distinction

BANCROFT: (Teut.) bean croft; (Ang.-Sax.) from the bean field

BANNISTER: (Gr.) the wild pomegranate

BARCA: (Pho.) lightning

BARDO: (Teut.) giant

BARLOW: (Celt.) a low branch; (Teut.) dweller on the boar's hill

BARRET, BARRETT: (Teut.) of bear strength

BARTH: (Old Eng.) a shelter

BARTIMEUS: (Heb.) of honourable lineage

BARTON: (Ang.-Sax.) a farmer

BARUCH: (Heb.) blessed

BAXTER: (Teut.) a baker

BAYARD: (Old Fr.) reddish-brown; he of the red hair

BEAUFORT: (Fr.) dweller in the fort

BEAUREGARD: (Fr.) fair of view; handsome

BEAVIS: (Eng.-Fr.) ox

BEDE: (Celt.) life; (Ang.-Sax.) prayer

BEDWIN: (Wel.) birch-like

BELA: (Heb.) eloquent

BELDEN: (Teut.) from a beautiful valley

BELEN: (Gr.) an arrow

BELI: (Wel.) bright

BELLAMY: (Lat.) beautiful friend

BELTHAM: (Teut.) comely

BELVA: (Lat.) fair

BENIAH: (Heb.) son of the Lord

BENTLEY: (Ang.-Sax.) from the winding grassy meadow

BENTON: (Ang.-Sax.) from the moor or meadow

BENVENUTO: (Lat.) welcome

BERENGER: (Teut.) bear-spear

BERGEN, BERGIN: (Teut.) dweller on the mountain

BERTHELM: (Ang.-Sax.) bright helmet

BERTHOLD: (Teut.) ruling in splendour

BETA: (Gr.) second letter of the Greek alphabet; second

BEVAN: (Celt.) son of Evan

BEVIS: (Teut.) a bow

BEYNON: (Wel.) son of Eynon

BIDDULPH: (Teut.) commanding wolf

BIMISI: (N.A. Ind.) slippery

BLEDDIAN, BLEDDYN: (Wel.) little wolf

BODEL: (Teut.) a herald

BOHDAN: (Slav.) God's gift

BOLESLAV: (Slav.) much glory

BONA: (Celt.) a messenger

BOURKE: (Teut.) a stronghold

BRADFORD: (Ang.-Sax.) from the broad ford

BRAM: a short form of Abraham

BRAN: (Celt.) a raven

BRENT: (Gr.) upright; (Ang.-Sax.) a steep hill

BRINSLEY: (Ang.-Sax.) Brin's meadow

BROCARD: (Teut.) badger's earth

BROCK: (Old Eng.) a badger

BRUIN: (Dutch) brown

BRYCHAN: (Wel.) speckled

BUCKLEY: (Ang.-Sax.) beech meadow

BURL: (Ang.-Sax.) a short form of Burleigh, town meadow

G

CADEYRN: (Wel.) battle king

CADFAEL: (Wel.) battle metal

CADMUS: (Gr.-Pho.) eastern

CADOGAN: (Wel.) little battle

CADOR: (Wel.) shield

CALVERT: (Ang.-Sax.) keeper of the calf-herd

CARBURY: (Celt.) charioteer

CAREW: (Cymric) castle near the water

CAREY: (Lat.) dear

CARLETON: (Ang.-Sax.) peasant's farm

CARNEY: (Celt.) brave soldier

CAROLAN: (Celt.) champion

CARRICK: (Celt.) a rocky headland

CASTOR: (Lat.) beaver

CATHAL: (Celt.) eye of battle

CAVANAGH, CAVANAUGH: (Celt.) handsome

CAVELL: (Teut.) active and bold

CEBAS: (Gr.) reverence

CEBERT: (Teut.) bright

CEDOMIL: (Slav.) a lover of children

CELYNEN: (Wel.) holly

CERI: (Wel.) loved one

CERWYN: (Wel.) fair love

CHALMERS: (Teut.) a chamberlain

CHANDLER: (Eng.) a merchant; (Lat.-Fr.) a candlemaker

CHELSEA: (Teut.) chalk port

CHESNEY: (Fr.) an oak grove

CHILWIN: (Gr.) perfect

CLARIDGE: (Teut.) illustrious

CLEDWYN: (Wel.) blessed sword

CLENTON: (Teut.) dweller on the summit

CLINTON: (Ang.-Sax.) from a farm on the headland

COEL: (Wel.) trust

COLBRAN: (Teut.) firebrand

COLGAR: (Celt.) proud warrior

COLLEY: (Ang.-Sax.) swarthy, black-haired

COLUMBUS: (Lat.) dove

CONROY: (Gael.) hound of the plain

COURTENAY, COURTNEY: (Teut.) dweller at the farm; (Fr.) a place-name

COVELL: (Old Eng.) wearer of a cowl

COWAN: (Scottish) a stone mason who has not served an apprenticeship

CRAMER: (Teut.) a merchant

CRAWFORD: (Old Eng.) from the crow's ford

CREON: (Old Eng.) accepted doctrine

CURRAN: (Celt.) hero

CURTIS: (Fr.) courteous

CURZON: (Teut.) a stump

CYNAN: (Wel.) chief

DAEGAL: (Scan.) a son born at dawn

DAIVA: (Sans.) a god in Irish mythology

DALBERT: (Teut.) from the bright valley

DALLAS: (Celt.) dweller in

the field near the waterfall

DALTON: (Ang.-Sax.) dweller in the vale near the village

DANTE: (Lat.) enduring

DARWIN: (Teut.) courageous friend; (Cymric) an oak

DEDAN: (Heb.) darling

DEDWYDD: (Wel.) happy

DELANO: (Erse) healthy, dark man; (Lat.-Fr.) aldergrove

DEMAS: (Lat.) respected

DEMPSEY: (Celt.) proud

DEMPSTER: (Old Eng.) wise as a judge

DENHAM: (Ang.-Sax.) from a home in the valley

DENMAN: (Ang.-Sax.) a man of the valley

DERBY: (Ang.-Sax.) the place of the deer

DERWENT: (origin unknown) a river name in England

DERWIN: (Ang.-Sax.) valued friend of the people

DESMO: (Gr.) a chain

DEVANEY: (Celt.) black strife

DEVARA: (Sans.) husband or lover

DEWAR: (Gael.) a pilgrim; (Celt.) heroic

DILWYN: (Teut.) calm friend

DINSMORE: (Teut.) the great fort

DONAGHAN: (Celt.) of dark complexion

DONATO: (Lat.) a gift

DONNELLY: (Celt.) brave, dark man

DORAN: (Gael.) a stranger

DORMAN: (Lat.) a sleeper

DORMAND: (Teut.) beloved protector

DOVEL: (Teut.) a young dove

DOYLE: (Celt.) dark stranger

DRUMMOND: (Celt.) dweller on the hill

DUAN(E): (Celt.) a poem or song

DUBERT: (Teut.) bright knight

DUDON: (Lat.) god-given

DUFF: (Gael.) dark-haired

DUNLEA: (Teut.) from the dark meadow

DURWIN: (Ang.-Sax.) dear friend

DUSTIN: (Teut.) a fighter

DYFAN: (Wel.) tribe ruler

DYFRIG: (Wel.) princely hero

DYNAMI: (N.A. Ind.) an eagle

DYNAND: (Cvmric) given

EATON: (Ang.-Sax.) from the riverside

EBERT: (Teut.) of active mind

EDBERT: (Ang.-Sax.) rich and generous

EDEN: (Heb.) delight

EDLIN, EDLUN: (Teut.-Ang.-Sax.) a nobleman of a prosperous village

EDMEAD: (Ang.-Sax.) noble reward

EDSEL: (Teut.) rich in self

EDWALD: (Teut.) rich in power

EGA: (Teut.) formidable

EGMONT: (Ang.-Sax.) sword protection; (Teut.) powerful protector; a famous Flemish patriot

EINAR: (Scan.) warrior chief; (Gr.) one who is sent

EIROS: (Wel.) bright

ELDORIS: (Teut.) spear-point

ELFED: (Wel.) autumn

ELFORD: (Teut.) dweller by the ford

ELIAN: (Lat.) brilliant

ELIKA: (Heb.) purified by God

ELIM: (Heb.) the oak

ELKI: (N.A. Ind.) bear

ELLERT: (Old Fr.) God's own gift

ELMEN: (Teut.) sturdy like an oak tree

ELRED: (Ang.-Sax.) noble counsel

ELROD: (Teut.) celebrated

ELROY: (Lat.) regal

ELVERT: (Lat.) variable

ELVIS: (Scan.) all-wise

ELWOOD: (Teut.) forest dweller

EMMET(T): (Lat.) industrious

EMYR: (Wel.) honour

ENAN: (Wel.) anvil; firm

ENEAS: (Gr.) worthy of praise

ENGELBERT: (Teut.) bright messenger

ENNIS: (Gr.) from Ennea; nine

ENOLD: (Teut.) the anointed

ENOS: (Heb.) man, mortal

ERBERT: (Teut.) always alert

ERHARD: (Teut.) intelligent resolution

ERLAND: (Teut.) foreign, from a foreign land

ERMIN: (Cymric) lordly

ESME: a Scottish use of the French Esmé, which is derived from the Latin, meaning esteemed

ETAM: (Lat.) of the warrior's house

ETENIA: (N.A. Ind.) wealthy

ETU: (N.A. Ind.) the sun

EUBULE: (Gr.) good counsellor

EUDON: (Gr.-Teut.) rich master

EUDORA: (Gr.) generous

EURWYN: (Wel.) golden fair

EVERALD: (Teut.) ever powerful

EZAR: (Heb.) treasure

FABRON: (Lat.) a man who works with his hands

FAIRBURN: (Teut.) comely child

FAIRHOLD: (Teut.) powerful

FARAMOND: (Teut.) travel protection

FARAND: (Teut.) attractive

FARMAN: (Teut.) traveller

FAXON: (Teut.) long-haired

FELIM: (Celt.) constantly good

FENNER: (Teut.) from the lowlands

FENWICK: (Teut.) from the marshland

FENWOOD: (Teut.) dweller in the lowlands forest

FERMIN: (Lat.) steadfast

FERNER: (Teut.) distant

FIDEL: (Lat.) faithful

FINDAL: (Teut.) inventive

FINDLAY: (Teut.) capable

FINNEGAN: (Celt.) fair

FLO: (N.A. Ind.) arrow-like

FLOBERT: (Teut.) of glorious fame

FLOREAN: (Lat.) flower beauty

FORTESCUE: (Teut.-Fr.) strong shield

FOSTER: (Old Eng.) a forester

FRITH: (Ang.-Sax.) dweller in the woodland

FRYSA: (Frie.) curly-haired

FULBERT: (Teut.) bright, shining

FULVIAN, FULVIUS: (Lat.) tawny

GADMAN(N): (Heb.) the fortunate one

GALEN: (Gr.) healer; probably named after the 2nd century Greek physician

GALVIN: (Celt.) sparrow

GARALT: (Teut.) brave warrior

GARDELL(E): (Teut.) a careful guard

GARFIELD: (Teut.) spear field

GARLAND: (Eng.-Fr.) crown, wreath

GAROLD: (Teut.) powerful warrior

GARVIN: (Teut.) warrior-friend

GAWAIN: a Welsh form of Gavin; (Celt.) hawk of battle

GAYNELL: (Teut.) one who profits

GELBERT: (Teut.) bright pledge

GEMMEL: (Scan.) old

GENESIUS: (Lat.) welcome newcomer

GENTILIS: (Lat.) the kind one

GERIUS: (Lat.) steadfast, constant

GERSHAM, GERSHOM: (Heb.) exiled

GERWYN: (Wel.) fair love

GETHIN: (Wel.) dark of skin

GILDAS: (Lat.-Gael.) servant of God

GILFORD: (Teut.) dweller by the big ford

GILLAND: (Teut.) bold youth

GLANMOR: (Wel.) seashore

GLEVE: (Teut.) point of a spear

GOLDWIN, GOLDWYN: (Ang.-Sax.) gold-friend

GOMEZ: (Span.-Teut.) man

GORMAN: (Teut.) man of clay

GOVERT: (Gr.) control

GRANVILLE: (Old Fr.) from the big city

GRATTAN: (Teut.) an enclosure

GREGG: (Teut.) increase

GRIMBALD: (Old Fr.) a bold son

GRISWOLD: (Teut.) from the wild forest

GRUFFYDD: (Wel.) strong warrior

GRUGWYN: (Wel.) white heather

GUILLYM: a Welsh form of William

GURIAS: (Heb.) of a nomadic family

GUTHRIE: (Celt.) war hero; (Ang.-Sax.) wise rule

GWERN: (Wel.) the alder tree

GWION: (Wel.) elf

GWYNFOR: (Wel.) a fair place

HAAKON: (Scan.) of high race

HABIB: (Syriac) beloved

HABOR: (Teut.) dexterous

HACHMANN: (Heb.) a learned man

HADDEN: (Old Eng.) of the moors

HADWIN: (Ang.-Sax.) family friend

HAFIZ: (Arab.) one who remembers

HAKAN: (N.A. Ind.) fiery

HALDANE, HALDEN: (Ang.-Scan.) half-Dane

HALLWORTH: (Old Norse) an amulet

HALMAR: (Scan.) helmet glory

HAMBLIN: (Teut.) crippled

HAMED: (Arab.) the praised

HAMFORD: (Teut.) from the black ford

HAMON: (Gr.) faithful

HANLEY: (Teut.-Ang.-Sax.) of the meadowland

HANNO: (Pho.) grace

HANSEL: (Heb.) God's grace

HAREM: (Heb.) a mountaineer

HARIM: (Heb.) flat-nosed

HARLAN(D): (Teut.) battle country

HARTMAN: (Teut.) the firm one

HASIN: (Sans.) laughter, laughing

HASSAN: (Arab.) handsome

HAVILAH: (Heb.) plentiful of treasure

HAZEN: (Teut.) a hare

HEATHCOAT, HEATHCOTT: (Ang.-Sax.) cottage on the heath

HEBERT: (Teut.) man of brilliance

HEILYN: (Wel.) cup-bearer

HELBERT: (Teut.) bright healer

HENDRY: (Teut.) manly

HENDY: (Teut.) skilful

HERVEY: (Celt.) progressive

HILDER: (Teut.) fighting man

HILLIARD: (Teut.) war guardian

HILTON: (Old Eng.) from the house on the hill

HINMAN: (Teut.) one who saves

HIROSHI: (Jap.) generous

HOLDEN: (Teut.) gracious, kind

HOLMAN(N): (Dutch) man of the hollow; (Teut.) from the river island

HOMER: (Gr.) pledge; (Ang.-Sax.) pool in a hollow

HOSEA: (Heb.) salvation; also related to Joshua

HOUGHTON: (Teut.) dweller at the hill estate

HOUSTON: (Ang.-Sax.) from a hill town

HOWLAND: (Old Eng.) of the hills

HULBERT: (Teut.) bright, faithful

HUME: (Teut.) home lover

HYWEL: (Wel.) eminent

IAGO: (Heb.) supplanter

IDDEN: (Ang.-Sax.) a prosperous man

IDDO: (Heb.) loving

IESTIN, IESTYN: (Wel.) the just; from the Latin, iustus

IEUAN: a Welsh form of John

IFOR: a Welsh form of Ivor

IGOR: (Scan.) hero

ILLTYD: (Wel.) ruler of a town or district

INIR: (Wel.) honour

IONWYN: (Wel.) fair lord

IRFON: (Wel.) the anointed one

ISA: (Gr.) equal

ISARD: (Teut.) inflexible as iron

ISMAN : (Heb.) faithful husband

ITHEL: (Wel.) generous lord

ITHNAN: (Heb.) the strong sailor

IVANDER: (Heb.) divine man

J

JABIN: (Heb.) born of God

JABRIEL: (Heb.) God-health

JADDA: (Heb.) man of wisdom

JAIR, JAIRUS: (Heb.) enlightened by God

JAKEH: (Heb.) pious

JANITRA: (Sans.) of high origin

JANUS: (Lat.) opener; sometimes given as two-faced, relating to the two-faced god of doors

JARRATT: (Teut.) firm combatant

JAVAS: (Sans.) swift

JEDIDIAH: (Heb.) beloved of the lord

JEHIAN: (Heb.) his life is Jehovah's

JEHOSHAPHAT: (Heb.) the Lord judges

JEPHUM: (Heb.) he is prepared

JORAM: (Heb.) the Lord is exalted

JOTHAM: (Heb.) the Lord is perfect

JOVIAN: (Lat.) of Jupiter

JUBALUS: (Lat.) lute-player

JUNIUS: (Lat.) of June; born in June

JURISA: (Slav.) storm

KALO: (Gr.) royal

KALON: (Gr.) noble

KAMPER: (Teut.) fighter
KEDAR: (Heb.) dark
KELBY: (Teut.) from a farm
KELSEY: (Teut.) from the water
KELWIN: (Celt.) dweller by the water
KENAZ: (Heb.) hunter
KENSELL: (Teut.) royally brave
KENWAY: (Ang.-Sax.) valiant soldier
KENYON: (Celt.) fair-haired
KILIAN: (Celt.) the innocent one
KIRBY: (Arab.) a waterskin; (Teut.) from the church village; (Eng.) English place name
KITTO: a pet form of Christopher
KYNAN: (Celt.) a form of Conal—daring all
KYNE: (Ang.-Sax.) bold

LABAN: (Heb.) white
LAIRD: (Celt.) landed proprietor
LARIS: (Lat.) cheerful
LATHA(A)M: (Teut.-Ang.-Sax.) of the village
LAWTON: (Old Eng.) a man of refinement
LAZAR: (Heb.) God will help
LEAR: (Celt.) calf-keeper; (Teut.) joyful
LEAVITT: (Ice.) a heritage
LEDGARD: (Teut.) national protector
LEDWIN: (Teut.) the nation's friend
LEE: (Teut.-Ang.-Sax.) a shelter, sheltered; also a variant of Lea (Lat.) a meadow
LELAND: (Ang.-Sax.) meadowland; from the meadowlands
LENNO: (N.A. Ind.) man

114

LEOFWIN: (Ang.-Sax.) dear friend

LEROY: (Old Fr.) the king

LEVIN: (Ang.-Sax.) valued friend

LINDO: (Teut.) lime tree; (Lat.) handsome

LINFRED: (Teut.) of gentle grace

LINGARD: (Teut.) gentle guard; (Celt.) the sea guard

LINUS: (Heb.) flaxen-haired

LINWOOD: (Eng.) lime wood

LLEUFER: (Wel.) splendid

LORUS: (Lat.) laurel

LUCANO: (Lat.) sunrise

LUKE: a variant of Lucas and Lucian (Lat.) light

LUMAN: (Lat.) radiant

LYCURGUS: (Gr.) the work of light

LYDELL: (Gr.) a Lydian; pertaining to Lydia in Asia Minor

LYMAN: (Ang.-Sax.) splendour; man of splendour

LYNFA: (Wel.) place of the lake

LYSANDER: (Gr.) liberator of men

M

MABON: (Wel.) youth

MACNAIR: (Gael.) son of the heir

MACY: (Old Eng.) sceptre bearer

MADDOCK, MADOC: (Celt.) fire; (Wel.) goodly, advantaged

MADISON: (Teut.) mighty in battle

MAELGWYN: (Wel.) metal-chief

MAGNA: (N.A. Ind.) the coming moon

MAHON: (Celt.) chief

MAITLAND: (Teut.) dweller in the meadowland; (Old Eng.) of the plains or meadows

MALCHUS: (Heb.) king

MALISE: (Gael.) servant of God, a disciple of Jesus

MALLARD: (Teut.) strong in counsel

MAL(L)ORY: (Lat.-Old Fr.) unfortunate, luckless

MALVIN: (Gael.) smooth brow; (Celt.) chief

MANDER: (Old Fr.) stable-boy

MANOAH: (Heb.) repose

MANSEL(L): (Wel.) a Norman place-name

MANUS: (Heb.) man at large; the public

MARCIUS: an early form of Mark; (Lat.) belonging to Mars

MARDON: (Teut.) famous master

MARIUS: (Lat.) of Mars; a disciplinarian

MARLAND: (Teut.) waste land

MARSDEN: (Teut.) valley of the combat; (Ang.-Sax.) from the marsh valley

MARTEL: (Old Fr.) war hammer

MARTIAL: (Lat.) pertaining to Mars, the god of war; warlike

MARVIN: (Teut.) warrior friend, or famous friend

MASKA: (N.A. Ind.) powerful

MATH: (Wel.) treasure

MEDWIN: (Teut.) strong or worthy friend

MELVERN: (N.A. Ind.) great chief

MERCER: (Lat.) merchant

MERRICK: (Teut.) renowned ruler

MERTON: (Ang.-Sax.) from near the sea

MERWIN, MERWYN: (Ang.-Sax.) famous friend

MILBURN: (Old Eng.) of the stream by the mill

MILLARD: (Ang.-Sax.) miller

MODRED: (Ang.-Sax.) brave advisor

MOELWYN: (Wel.) fair-haired

MORDAUNT: (Lat.) biter

MORDEYRN: (Wel.) great monarch

MORELL, MORRELL: (Lat.-Teut.) dark, swarthy

MORTON: (Ang.-Sax.) from the moor village

MORYS: a Welsh form of Maurice

MOSTYN: (Wel.) field fortress

MUNRO, MUNROSE: see Monroe

MYLOR: (Celt.) prince

NAAMAN(N): (Heb.) agreeable, pleasant one

NADABB: (Heb.) he of broad ideas

NALDO: (Teut.) the valiant one

NAPOLEON: (Gr.-Lat.) one who belongs to the new city

NARCISSUS: (Gr.) daffodil; in mythology a youth enamoured with his own image

NATHAN: (Heb.) a gift

NEEDHAM: (Teut.) home tyrant

NENNOG: (Wel.) heavenly one

NETIS: (N.A. Ind.) trusted friend

NEVLIN: (Celt.) sailor

NEWBERN: (Teut.) new chief

NEWBOLD: (Old Eng.) of the new building

NEWCOMB: (Ang.-Sax.) a stranger

NEWLIN: (Teut.) new arrival

NEWTON: (Ang.-Sax.) of the new town or estate

NIAL(L): (Celt.) champion

NICANDER: (Gr.) man of victory

NICO: (Gr.) victory

NICODEMUS: (Gr.) the people's victor

NICOMEDE: (Gr.) victorious ruler

NIGER: (Lat.) black

NILS: a Scandinavian form of Neil

NINIAN: (Celt.-Lat.) thought to be a corruption of Vivian; formerly in use in Scotland

NODAS: (Heb.) noble son of the Lord

NODIN: (N.A. Ind.) wind

NOLAN(D): (Gael.) noble

NORTON: (Ang.-Sax.) from the north place or part

NORVIN: (Teut.) man from the north

NORWOOD: (Teut.) literally, north wood; dweller at the north gate or forest

NOTOS: (Gr.) the south wind

NOVA: (Lat.) new

O

OAKLEY: (Teut.-Ang.-Sax.) dweller at the oak meadow

OBED: (Heb.) serving, worshipper (of God)

OBERT: (Teut.) illustrious

OCTAVIUS: (Lat.) eighth

ODAGOMA: (N.A. Ind.) iron nerve

ODALRIC: (Teut.) rich ruler

ODEL, ODELL: (Norse) man of a rich estate

ODELON: (Teut.) rich, wealth

ODMAR: (Teut.) rich man of fame

ODMUND: (Teut.) rich protector

ODOLF: (Teut.) wise rich man

ODON: (Teut.) rich master

ODWIN: (Teut.) rich friend

OGDEN: (Ang.-Sax.) from the oak valley

OGMUND: (Teut.) awesome protector

OLA: (Heb.) eternity

OLAVE: (Norse) ancestor's relic

OLCOTT: (Teut.) dweller in the old cottage

OLEN: (Teut.) inheritor

OLVIDIO (Span.) forgetful

OMAN: (Scan.) high protector

OMANISA: (N.A. Ind.) wanderer

ONESIMUS: (Gr.) beneficial

ONLLWYN: (Wel.) ash-grove

ONORATO: (Lat.) honoured

OPIE: (Gr.) opium

ORAN: (Irish) a wren; sometimes used in Ireland for Ádrian

OREL: (Lat.) the listener

OREN: (Heb.) the pine tree

ORIEN: (Lat.) sunrise

ORLANDO: an Italian form of Roland

ORLIN: (Gr.-Lat.) golden brightness

ORLON: (Teut.) rich

ORO: (It.) gold

ORRA: (origin unknown) unmatched, odd

ORRICK: (Teut.) golden rule

ORRIS: (Old Fr.) a certain kind of gold or silver lace

ORTENSIO: (Lat.) gardener

ORTWIN: (Teut.) rich friend

ORVILLE: (Old Fr.) lord of the estate; (man of) the rich town

ORWIN: (Teut.) golden friend

OSFRED: (Teut.) divine power

OSGOOD: (Teut.) divinely good

OSLAC: (Teut.) divine sport

OSMER: (Teut.) divinely famed

OSRIC: (Teut.) divine ruler

OSWIN: (Ang.-Sax.) divine friend

OSWYTH: (Teut.) divine strength

OTADAN: (N.A. Ind.) plenty

OTIS: (Gr.) keen hearing

OTTE: (Teut.) happy

OTWAY, OTTWAY: (Teut.) lucky warrior

OTWEL: (Teut.) instrument of dread

OURAY: (N.A. Ind.) an arrow

OUTRAM: (Teut.) honoured warrior

OZUL: (Heb.) a shadow

PACIAN: (Lat.) man of peace

PACO: (N.A. Ind.) bold eagle

PADARN: (Wel.) fatherly

PADMA: (Sans.) flower of the lotus

PAGET: (Old Fr.) little page associated with pageantry

PAINE: (Lat.) man of the country

PAISLEY: (Lat.) yield of the country

PAKAVI: (N.A. Ind.) a reed

PALLATON: (N.A. Ind.) fighter

PALMER: (Lat.-Ang.-Sax.) pilgrim

PARK: (Chin.) the cypress tree

PATE: (Gael.) noble; (Eng. usage) crown of the head; a Scottish version of Patrick

PATERA: (Sans.) a bird

PATTRA: (Sans.) pinion of a wing

PATU: (Sans.) a protector

119

PATWIN: (N.A. Ind.) a man

PAWLEY: an old English variant of Paul

PAX: (Lat.) peace

PAXTON: (Teut.) a traveller from a distant part

PAYTON: (Ang.-Sax.) St Patrick's town

PELEG: (Heb.) a division

PELEX: (Gr.) a warrior's helmet

PENN: (Ang.-Sax.) enclosure

PENROD: (Wel.) top of the ford

PENROSE: (Celt.) one who lives at the head of the moor; an English placename

PENWYN: (Wel.) fair head

PERSEUS: (Gr.) destroyer; fabled Greek hero who slew Medusa

PETROS: (Gr.) of stone

PEVERIL: (Lat.) boyish

PHAO: (Gr.) giver of light

PHAON: (Gr.) brilliant

PHARAMOND: (Teut.) journey protection

PHARAOH: (Egyp.) the sun

PHAROS: (Gr.) a beacon

PENDLETON: (Cymric) derived from an English town named after its rock outcrops

PHELAN: (Celt.) wolf; sometimes considered a good luck omen

PHILANDER: (Gr.) a man who loves all mankind

PHILARET: (Gr.) a lover of virtue

PHILEMON: (Gr.) a kiss

PHILETAS, PHILETUS: (Gr.) beloved

PHILIBERT: (Teut.) very bright

PHILO: (Gr.) love

PHOEBUS: (Gr.) the shining one

PIERREPONT: (Fr.) stone bridge

PIERSON: (Fr.) son of Pierre

PIUS: (Lat.) dutiful

PLATO: (Gr.) broad; broad-shouldered; name of famous Greek philosopher

PLAUDO: (Lat.) one who is worthy of praise; applauded

POLDO: (Teut.) the people's prince

POLLARD: (Teut.) the un-afraid

POMROY: (Lat.) apple king; (Old Fr.) apple orchard

POWA: (N.A. Ind.) rich

POWELL: (Celt.) alert

POWYS: (Wel.) a man from Powis

PRESCOTT: (Ang.-Sax.) the priest's house

PRESTON: (Ang.-Sax.) the priest's village

PRIMUS: (Lat.) first

PRIYA: (Sans.) beloved

PROBERT: (Teut.) brilliance

PROBUS: (Lat.) honest

PROCTOR: (Lat.) leader

PROSPER, PROSPERO: (Lat.) prosperous

PROTEUS: (Gr.) changeful

PURDY: (Hin.) a recluse

PURVANCE: (Slav.) the first

PWYLL: (Wel.) prudence

QUARTUS: (Lat.) fourth

QUINCY: (Teut.) a dialectic form of whence; (Fr.) a place name

QUINN: (Gael.) counsel

RAB: (Teut.) bright fortune

RADBERT: (Teut.) bright counsellor

RADMAN: (Slav.) joy

RAE: (Teut.) a roe

RAFE: a phonetic form of Ralph

RAGMAR: (Teut.) wise warrior

RAGNOLD: (Teut.) powerful judge

RAINER: (Teut.) prudent warrior

RALEIGH: (Teut.) dweller at the roe meadow; (Eng.) from the hunting lodge

RAMA: (Sans.) bringer of joy

RAMAH: (Heb.) a lofty place; (Lat.) a brand

RAMBERT: (Teut.) bright raven

RANALD: (Teut.) powerful counsel; a variant of Ronald

RANDER: (Teut.) home-lover

RANSOME: (Middle Eng.) redemption

RAOUL: (Teut.) helpful commander

RASMUS: form of Erasmus, — the desired

RATHBONE: (Old Fr.) dweller at the river fort

RATHBURN: (Teut.) dweller at the running brook

RAVELIN: (Lat.) a rampart

RAWDON: (Teut.) a red roe

RAYNALD: (Teut.) of firm judgment

RAYO: (Teut.) a beam of light

READ, READE: (Teut.) ruddy; red-haired

REBA: (Heb.) a quarter

REECE: (Teut.) swift; an English form of Rhys

REEVE, REEVES: (Old Eng.) high official of a district; a bailiff or steward

REGAN: (Celt.) royal, king

REGULUS: (Lat.) a little king

REINALDO: (Teut.) pure and brave

REINGARD: (Teut.) incorruptible guard

REINHART: (Teut.) of incorruptible firmness; staunch

REMUS: (Lat.) fair

REMY: (Lat.) an oarsman

RENARD: (Teut.) of firm decision

RENAUD: (Old Fr.) powerful judgment

RENAULD: (Lat.) reborn

RENFRED: (Teut.) wise and peaceful judgment

REVEL: (Heb.) a shepherd; (Lat.) joy

REXFORD: (Teut.) from the king's ford

REXWALD: (Teut.) of kingly power

REYHAN: (Arab.) the favoured of a deity

REYNER: (Lat.) kingly

REZON: (Heb.) prince

RHAIN: (Wel.) a lance
RHESA: (Chaldaic) prince
RHODES: (Gr.) roses
RHONWEN: (Wel.) slender and fair
RHUN: (Wel.) grand
RIDDELL: (Old Eng.) a sieve
RIDLEY: (Teut.) dweller on the dark ridge; (Old Eng.) dweller by the red field
RILEY: (Old Eng.) turbid, disorderly
RIMMON: (Heb.) thunderer
RIORDAN: (Celt.) royal bard
RITCHIE: (Teut.) firm ruler
ROALD: (Teut.) famed power
ROB: see Robert
RODMUND: (Teut.) famous protector
ROHIN: (Sans.) one who follows the upward path
ROMEO: (It.) a pilgrim to Rome
ROMERO: (Lat.) a wanderer
ROMOLO: (Teut.) fame
RONDELL: (It.) plump, round
ROSCOE: (Teut.) sea horse
ROSPERT: (Teut.) bright horse
ROSSER: (Celt.) champion

ROWAN: (Celt.) famous
ROWE: (Ang.-Sax.) rest
ROY: (Celt.) red
ROYDEN: (Teut.) dweller in the king's glen
RUBIN: (Lat.) a ruby
RUFORD, RUFFORD: (Old Eng.) of the red ford
RULAND: (Teut.) famed in the land
RULIFF: (Teut.) fortunate
RYAN: (Lat.) laughing

SAADI: (Pers.) wise
SABIAN: (Heb.) host of heaven
SABINE: (Lat.) a tribal name
SABU: (Hin.) follower of a tribe
SAD: (Celt.) the just
SADOC: (Heb.) sacred

SAHALE: (N.A. Ind.) above

SAIRE: (Teut.) hermit

SAKIMA: (N.A. Ind.) king

SALADIN: (Arab.) goodness of the faith

SAMA: (Sans.) tranquillity

SAMULA: (Sans.) foundation

SANCHIA: (Span.) holy

SANDFORD: (Ang.-Sax.) a sandy ford or crossing

SANFRED: (Teut.) peaceful counsel

SANSON: (Heb.) brilliant sun

SANUYA: (N.A. Ind.) cloud

SAPATA: (N.A. Ind.) hugging bear

SARID: (Heb.) a survivor

SAVA: (Heb.) repose

SAVERO: (Arab.) bright

SAWA: (N.A. Ind.) rock

SAXON: (Teut.) rock; (Ang.-Sax.) short-sword warrior

SAYRES: (Teut.) conquering host

SCHOLEM: (Heb.) peace

SCHUYLER: (Dutch) a place of shelter; a shelterer

SCIPIO: (Lat.) a staff

SEADON: (Old Eng.) one who lives in the field near the sea

SEAN, SHAWN: an Irish form of John—Jehovah has favoured; the Lord graciously giveth

SEARLE, SEARLES: (Teut.) a wearer of armour

SEATON: (Teut.) one who lives on an estate near the sea

SEAVER: (Ang.-Sax.) of the victorious stronghold

SEBA: (Gr.) venerated

SEBERT: (Ang.-Sax.) famous in victory

SECUNDO: (Lat.) the second

SEDGWICK: (Ang.-Sax.) sedgy (reedy) village

SEFTON: (Old Eng.) after the place-name in England

SEIF: (Arab.) the sword of religion

SELAS: (Gr.) a bright flame

SELDON: (Teut.) rare

SELED: (Heb.) the leaper

SELFRIDGE: (Teut.) lord of the ridge

SELIG, ZELIG: (Teut.) blessed

SELMAR: (Lat.) the rolling sea

SELVAC: (Celt.) rich in cattle

SELWYN: (Ang.-Sax.) blessed friend

SEMA: (Gr.) a sign from heaven

SEVER: (Lat.) austere

SEWARD: (Ang.-Sax.) victory protection; (Teut.) warden of the sea coast

SEWELL: (Ang.-Sax.-Teut.) victorious rule

SHALLUM: (Heb.) perfect

SHAPONDA: (N.A. Ind.) passing through

SHAW: (Teut.) from a shady grove

SHEM: (Heb.) name; renown

SHERARD: (Teut.) splendidly brave

SHERLOCK: (Teut.) fairhaired; (Middle Eng.) shorn head

SHERMAN: (Ang.-Sax.) a wool shearer

SHERWIN: (Ang.-Sax.) a true friend

SHERWOOD: (Celt.) sea ruler; (Ang.-Sax.) bright forest

SHIRA: (Heb.) welfare

SIBOLD: (Teut.) conquering prince

SIDNEY, SYDNEY: (Teut.) of St Denys

SIEBERT: (Teut.) bright conqueror

SIEGFRIED: (Teut.) victorious peace

SIEVER: (Scan.) victorious guard

SIGMUND: (Teut.) victorious protector

SILABU: (N.A. Ind.) a falcon

SILEO: (Teut.) conquering messenger

SILSBY: (Old Eng.) of the forest farm

SILVA: (Lat.) of the forest

SIM, SIMEON: (Heb.) obedient; hearkening

SINCLAIR: (Lat.) saintly; illustrious

SIVA: (Heb.) propitious

SLOANE: (Celt.) fighter, warrior

SOFIAN: (Arab.) devoted

125

SOL: (Lat.) the sun; also diminutive of Solomon

SOLON: (Gr.) wisdom

SONGAN: (N.A. Ind.) string

SORLE: (Teut.) armour

SPIRO: (Gr.) breath of the gods

SPRAGUE: (Dutch) eloquent; (Old Eng.) the alert one

STANFIELD: (Ang.-Sax.) stony field

STANFORD: (Ang.-Sax) stony crossing

STARR: (Teut) inflexible

STEIN: (Teut.) stone

STEINHART: (Teut.) stony; unyielding

STODDARD: (Ang.-Sax.) keeper of horses; (Old. Fr.) a peaceful man

STURGES: (Gr.) natural affection; parental love

SULIEN: (Wel.) sun-born

SULLIVAN: (Celt.) blue-eyed

SULWYN: (Wel.) sun-fair

SUTA: (N.A. Ind.) tough

SWEYN: (Ang.-Sax.) servant; swineherd

SYENA: (Sans.) hawk, falcon

SYLGWYN: (Wel.) Whitsun

TADEO: (Aramaic) praise

TAMA: (N.A. Ind.) a thunderbolt

TEDMAN: (Teut.) patriot

TESMOND: (Teut.) a protector from evil

TEVIS: (Old Eng.) a shilling

THORBERT: (Teut.) Thor's thunder

THORPE: (Teut.) from a village

TIBAL: (Teut.) people's prince

TIERNAN: (Celt.) kingly

TIMON: (Gr.) honourable

TITUS: (Lat.) saved, safe

TORBERT: (Teut.) bright eminence

TRAVIS: (Teut.) uniting; (Fr.) crossroads

TUDOR: (Celt.) divine gift
TUDWAL: (Wel.) tribe wall
TYNDALL: (Ang.-Sax.) an everburning light
TYSON: (Teut.) son of the German

ULAND: (Teut.) from a noble land
ULRICA: (Nor.) ruler
ULTANN: (Wel.) saintly
UNNI: (Heb.) modest
UPTON: (Ang.-Sax.) town on the heights
URIEN: (Wel.) town-born

VALDIS: (Teut.) lively in battle

VIRGIL: (Lat.) flourishing
VOLNEY: (Teut.) popular
VYCHAN: (Wel.) little

WALSTAN: (Ang.-Sax.) wall-stone; corner-stone
WILDON: (Ang.-Sax.) curving valley
WINSLOW: (Teut.) from the friendly hill
WINTHROP: (Ang.-Sax.) from the friendly village
WYATT: (Fr.) a guide
WYSTAND: (Ang.-Sax.) battle stone

XENOPHON: (Gr.) strange-sounding
XERXES: (Pers.) king

Y

Z

YALE: (Teut.) one who pays

YATES: (Ang.-Sax.) one who guards the gate

YNYR: (Wel.) honour

YVES: (Scan.) an archer

ZENO: (Gr.) stranger

ZELIG: (Teut.) blessed